CONCEPT BOO

THINKING AB

GW01460330

CONCEPT BOOKS

General Editor: Alan Harris

THINKING ABOUT
EDUCATION

ALAN HARRIS

HEINEMANN EDUCATIONAL
BOOKS LONDON

Heinemann Educational Books Ltd
LONDON   EDINBURGH   MELBOURNE
JOHANNESBURG   AUCKLAND
TORONTO   SINGAPORE   NEW DELHI
IBADAN   HONG KONG   NAIROBI

ISBN 0 435 46189 3

Published in Great Britain by
Heinemann Educational Books Ltd
48 Charles Street, London W1X 8AH
Printed by Cox & Wyman Ltd
London, Reading and Fakenham

Contents

To Monica Perkins
who despite this book will never be able to write

Preface

THIS book is aimed mainly at sixthformers and at students beginning courses in Colleges of Education; but I hope that teachers and parents will also find it of interest.

It is primarily concerned with the *philosophy* of education in that it deals with conceptual questions about aims and values; but readers are also shown the relevance of other disciplines such as Psychology and Sociology.

The first part of the book, 'Education and the Curriculum', is basically concerned with the *content* of what we teach in schools: the second part, 'Education and Values', is more concerned with how we can *justify* what we teach and how we teach it.

Students tend to feel that philosophy is remote from the 'real' problems of the classroom. In an attempt to convince them otherwise I have included some relevant interludes concerning Blackmore Secondary Modern School and its more progressive neighbour, Blackmore County Primary School.

These are, of course, imaginary institutions. If readers recognize any of the characters involved this may possibly be mere coincidence.

Acknowledgements

OF the many people who have helped me in the writing of this book I would particularly like to thank the following: Eric Smith (for his comments as one concerned with the training of teachers), Michael Morris (for his comments as a teacher), Dr Jean Harris (for her help with psychological issues), Mrs Valerie Denman (for her comments as a student teacher), and Howell Jones.

The Author and Publishers wish to thank the following for permission to reprint copyright material:

Mrs Laura Huxley and Chatto & Windus for an extract from *Brave New World* by Aldous Huxley; Her Majesty's Stationery Office for an extract from the *Plowden Report*; Robert Graves for 'The Cool Web', from *Collected Poems* 1965; The Church Information Office for an extract from *Sex Education in Schools*. Dr Otto Frank and Vallentine, Mitchell for an extract from *The Diary of Anne Frank*; The Religious Education Association, New York, for an extract from 'Comparative Study of Religion in Schools', published in *Religious Education,* Jan.–Feb. 1969; Professor P. H. Hirst for an extract from 'Morals, Religion and the Maintained Schools', published in the *British Journal of Educational Studies.*

PART ONE

Education and the Curriculum

one

What is Education?

EDUCATION is not a 'subject' in any simple sense. One does not talk of 'learning' Education in the same way that one talks of learning Mathematics or learning History.

In a College of Education students will learn one or two main subjects (say Art, or English) and they will also take a course in Education. In this course they will consider *aims* in education, *methods* of achieving these aims, and the *theories* which relate both to aims and methods. And they will learn *facts* (especially under the headings of Psychology and Sociology) which are relevant to their work as teachers. The course will help students to answer quite different types of question, concerning *aims* (What should we try to achieve as teachers? What makes one sort of curriculum more worth while than another?), *methods* (How can one get children interested in this subject? What is the most effective way of teaching infants to read? What kind of discipline really works in a secondary school?) and *theories* (Does streaming result in poorer work from the weakest pupils? How do children form mathematical concepts? What is the relationship between social class and academic potential?)

Seen in this light, Education is more akin to a field such as psychiatry than to a subject such as Maths or History. In psychiatry too there are problems of method and theory on one hand, and of aim on the other. The *aim* of psychiatry is to promote mental health, and here the main problem is to define what one *means* by mental health. This is a much more difficult problem than one might at first think. For example, in one society it might be regarded as normal for men to be aggressive and domineering,

whereas another society might regard aggressiveness as an un-
healthy trait. Another example concerns homosexuality. Is it
'healthy' in any given case for a person to be homosexual, or is this
a condition that should be 'cured'? The psychiatrist must leave
this decision to the homosexual himself, but indirectly the specific
nature of his aim (mental health) is bound to be conditioned by
the culture of the society in which he works. At least part of the
concept of mental health involves satisfactory 'adjustment'
to one's environment, but what if the environment itself is sick?
Liberally-minded people living in Nazi Germany seldom wished
to become happily adjusted to the atrocitics taking place around
them.

It is easier to describe the *methods* of psychiatry than to define
its aims. For example these include 'physical' techniques like the
use of drugs and 'non-physical' techniques like psycho-analysis;
there is a vast literature describing these techniques in great detail.
But it is not so easy to *explain* these methods or even to prove that
they are effective. There are many *theories* concerning psycho-
analysis (one talks of different schools of psychotherapy) but few,
if any, of these theories can be proved scientifically. Sometimes
psycho-analysts who hold incompatible theories use much the
same methods with much the same results, and the same thing
applies to educational theories, as we shall see later.

Sometimes methods of treatment are discovered by chance (like
the use of electroconvulsive therapy to help patients suffering from
acute depression) and then attempts are made to find a theoretical
explanation for *why* the method works. Less often, doctors will
develop a theory (like 'behaviourism') and then predict the effects
of a method of treatment (like aversion therapy). (Similarly, certain methods of teaching reading were investigated *after* psychologists had developed certain learning theories.) It is far more
common, however, for successful methods to be evolved before
they can be accounted for theoretically – and this is because,
generally speaking, the social sciences are much less precise than,
say, Physics or Chemistry, which provide a very sound theoretical
basis for professions such as engineering and agriculture.

This digression about psychiatry will perhaps shed some light on similar questions concerning Education.

The main *aim* of educators is to produce educated people; but the problems of defining 'educated' are even more difficult than those of defining 'healthy'. The popular concept of 'educated' will vary from society to society and in any one place from generation to generation. Without going into detail at this stage there are clearly many differences between the educational ideals reflected by early British Public Schools and those reflected by modern comprehensives. And there is a sharp contrast between the educational ideals of a democracy (such as the U.S.A.) and those of a totalitarian state (such as communist China) – the former, at least in principle, placing value on freedom of political thinking, the latter valuing uncritical loyalty and the subservience of individual desires to the welfare of the 'State'.

It is worth noting that however much the concept of 'educated' or 'healthy' may vary from place to place, nobody nowadays is likely to *disapprove* of these qualities. It would be very odd to say 'Smith is a pleasant chap but he's educated' or 'Jones is a good man but he's sane'. In special cases there might be some significance in saying that someone was 'too educated' (meaning perhaps that he kept showing off intellectually) or 'too sane' (meaning that he lacked a sense of humour). But logically it is necessarily *good* to be educated and *good* to be healthy and sane.

Both education and health are ends in themselves. One doesn't *need* to justify good health by saying 'It enables me to do my job' or 'I can care for my family better if I'm fit'. It makes sense to cultivate good health for its own sake, irrespective of what other benefits are achieved. Similarly one does not need to justify education by saying that it helps you to earn more money or to play a more useful role in society. Education is desirable for its own sake.

Professor R. S. Peters, discussing the concepts of 'education' and 'reform', stresses that they do not name any specific kind of process, 'They are more like stamps of approval issued by *Good Housekeeping* proclaiming that furniture has come up to standard.'

The fact that the term 'educated' involves a value judgement is of the utmost importance in discussing educational aims and methods. It follows that what is *learnt* should in some sense be worth while (it would be odd to talk of being *educated* in astrology or Bingo) and it also follows, though less obviously, that the methods used by teachers should be morally acceptable (it would not count as an *educational* process to brainwash children and indoctrinate them with certain beliefs, even if the beliefs were correct). And the 'stamp of approval' nature of the word education helps to distinguish it from words like 'training' and 'instruction'. One could be trained to exterminate Jews, but not *educated* to do so. One could be given instruction in History, but this implies less than being *educated* in History.

Both training and instruction (the former developing skills and the latter factual knowledge) can be very important elements of education but they are not equivalent to it. A man may be a skilled driver or computer-operator without being *educated* in mechanical or mathematical principles, and a man may be 'well-informed' about the news without understanding its significance. 'Education' involves the understanding of *principles* as well as the acquisition of skills or information.

Furthermore it would be odd to describe a man as educated, however brilliant a doctor or engineer he might be, if he were still a baby emotionally. Education proper deeply involves the whole personality, whereas training and instruction need touch only the surface of the mind.

We might also deny the stamp of approval to a man who was brilliant at his own job but who was totally ignorant in all other respects. Being educated suggests an all-round achievement rather than narrow specialization.

Professor Peters* summarizes these points as follows:

(1) An educated man is one whose form of life – as exhibited in his conduct, the activities to which he is committed, his judgements and feelings – is thought to be desirable.

* *The Concept of Education,* ed. Peters, Allen & Unwin.

(2) Whatever he is trained to do he must have knowledge, not just knack, and an understanding of principles. His form of life must also exhibit some mastery of forms of thought and awareness which are not harnessed purely to utilitarian or vocational purposes or completely confined to one mode.

(3) His knowledge and understanding must not be inert . . . in the sense that they make no difference to his general view of the world.

Professor Peters is here stressing that 'educated' suggests certain value judgements rather than names specific abilities or a specific range of knowledge. The expression 'having good dress sense' functions in the same sort of way, for to say that a man is well-dressed is to express approval without saying what he is actually wearing. However, in a specific social context 'well-dressed' would in fact suggest some specific details. In this country one could predict roughly what would be worn by a 'well-dressed' middle-class man at a dinner party, or by a rural G.P. going his rounds. In the same way there are detailed expectations, in a given society, of what educated people will have studied and what sort of training they will have had. Thus an educated Englishman in the nineteenth century would know Latin and Greek, would have been trained for a profession (Church, Army, Law, etc.) and to some extent would have predictable attitudes concerning religion, patriotism, politics, etc. (Perhaps the reader could draw up his own list of what would be expected of an educated woman in the time of Jane Austen, and of an educated business executive nowadays.)

The danger of thinking in terms of the 'content' of education is that one may confuse the content with education itself. A man may have been to Eton, qualified as a doctor, learned to play the violin, and so on, without being *educated*, just as a person wearing fashionable clothes need not necessarily have good dress sense. And teachers who concentrate on content rather than on education will *instruct* rather than educate.

To conclude this chapter, here is a list of commonly accepted

B

aims in education, drawn up by Professor D. J. O'Connor*:

(1) to provide men and women with a minimum of skills neces-
    sary for them (a) to take their place in society, and (b) to seek
    further knowledge;
(2) to provide them with a vocational training that will enable
    them to be self-supporting;
(3) to awaken an interest in and a taste for knowledge;
(4) to make them critical;
(5) to put them in touch with and train them to appreciate the
    cultural and moral achievements of mankind.

It would be an interesting exercise to say precisely what sort of
educational curriculum would be involved under these five headings in (a) a primitive tribe subsisting by fishing and hunting, (b)
Greece at the time of Plato, and (c) technologically backward
Britain in the year A.D. 2000.

Conclusion

Education involves practical methods of achieving certain aims.
This chapter has mainly been concerned with *aims*. It has been
stressed that these aims are intimately bound up with value judgements which in turn are bound up with the culture of the society
providing the education. Some later chapters will be concerned
with *method* and *theory*. Meanwhile readers may like to consider
the staff meeting at Blackmore Secondary Modern School (pp
9–12) and see if they can sort out, at this stage, which parts of the
argument are concerned with educational *aims*, as opposed to
methods or theory.

---

* *An Introduction to the Philosophy of Education*, O'Connor, R.K.P.

Interlude 1

IN Blackmore Secondary Modern School a special staff meeting was called to discuss the following year's syllabus for 4C – the pupils who would be leaving without taking exams of any kind.

The Headmaster was very concerned about 4C. Most of his teaching career had been in Grammar schools, where the majority of pupils tended to do what work they were told to do even if it was pointless and boring. When he took a headship in a secondary modern (hoping it would turn into a Comprehensive school and give him more prestige) he found that with regard to the 'A' stream things were reassuringly familiar. Indeed, he was impressed by the success rate in 'O-level', and by the atmosphere of the newly created 6th form.

But when he first encountered 4C, to teach them General English for two periods a week, he was out of his depth. An early incident was when he set the class to write an essay on 'The Pleasures of Winter', and Monica Perkins (famous for her Irish boy-friends from the local building site) assured him, 'If you lived in my bleeding house, the only bleeding pleasure you'd get in winter would be to go to bed with a bottle of bleeding gin.'

(This is what educational psychologists call a 'restricted linguistic code', but the Headmaster didn't know this and was deeply offended.)

Shortly after this episode he decided that pressures of administration didn't really leave him time to teach 'C' stream classes; consequently 4C General English was taken over by Miss Gifkins, straight from college, and the Head happily taught 5A how to write intelligent Eng. Lit. essays about G.C.E. plays that they had never seen.

Meanwhile, Miss Gifkins, who believed in getting children to write about Real Life, set Monica the task of writing an essay on 'The Pleasures of Drinking Gin in Bed', only to discover that the girl could neither read nor write.

*   *   *

Fortunately there were some excellent teachers in the school who were determined to make some sort of sense out of 4C's timetable, which up till now had been exactly the same as 4A's.

At the staff meeting Mrs Bryce, the deputy head, made the point that 4C was always a badly behaved, restless class mainly because they *were* 4C. 'If you grade children A, B and C,' she said, 'the "C"-streamers will eventually give up and *behave like* "C"-streamers. And the longer they are in the "C" stream the worse they'll get.'

Several teachers supported the view that the school should begin to 'unstream', starting with the first year and then, year by year, developing mixed ability groups throughout the school. Other teachers argued that it would be impossible to teach mixed-ability groups – the brighter pupils would fall behind, the atmosphere would deteriorate: 'How can you teach "O-level" to a class when some of them can hardly read?' To which the progressives replied that new teaching methods would be needed: the brighter pupils would help the slower ones; one could no longer lecture at the whole class but would have to divide one's time between small groups, each working at its own pace.

4C's former teacher supported Mrs Bryce, but pointed out that this was long-term policy. The immediate problem was to work out a suitable syllabus for the coming year. The head of the wood-work department launched into an attack on 'frills' like literature, R.E. and Art. 'These kids aren't going to read *books*,' he said. 'They aren't going to write *essays*. They're going to be labourers and shop assistants. So let's spend the year teaching them what they *need* to know. Carpentry, metalwork and bit of General Science for the boys. Enough English and Maths for them to understand hire-purchase forms. Cookery and dressmaking for the girls, and lessons on how to use make-up and dress decently. Enough oral English to speak clearly behind the counter at Woolworths, and enough Maths to give customers the right change.'

This point of view was vociferously supported by several of the staff, who added topics like plumbing, interior decoration, child care and birth control ('to stop the little so-and-so's multiplying like rabbits', as Mr Rees-Jones put it). The Headmaster was shocked at the last suggestion, but began to see the light – of course, what people like Monica Perkins needed was *vocational* training.

But the liberals on the staff objected very much to this attitude. The R.E. teachers talked at length about spiritual values and the English staff about self-expression. Miss Gifkins threw in some remarks about child-centred education, but everyone ignored her. Many of the staff deeply distrusted the modern Colleges of Education, whose lecturers were out of touch with life in the classroom, and Miss Gifkins did nothing to reassure them with remarks like 'Successful role-play is an essential feature of self-actualization' (which was her argument for letting Jimmy Mordey, a noted delinquent, be milk monitor for 1 C).

Mr Brown (Social Studies) said that it was essential to prepare pupils for their place in a democracy. This was more important in the last year than vocational training (which they would have *anyway* when they left school). 'How can you have a true democracy when three-quarters of the population are totally ignorant of local government. No wonder elections in this country are a farce.' The Headmaster began to see light again – of course, pupils must be prepared for their role in democracy. A good point for Speech Day. A sound balance between practical work, English, Maths, R.E. and Current Affairs was obviously called for – pretty much the same sort of timetable as already existed, in fact.

Mr Bennett (4C) began to get extremely irritated. 'Look,' he said, 'it doesn't matter a damn what *subjects* they have on the timetable. What matters is *how* we teach the kids. We've got to stop treating them like overgrown school children and start treating them like young adults. Half the girls will be married within three years of leaving school: they're *women*. And all we do is make them sing "All things bright and beautiful" and give them piddling essays to write.'

The Headmaster gave him a dirty look and asked if he had any constructive suggestions to make.

'Yes, I've got several. First, I want to turn their classroom into a work room. Get rid of the baby desks and use ordinary tables and chairs. I want to take over the old changing rooms to use as a common room, where they can brew their own coffee and spend their free periods . . .'

Miss Smithson (Domestic Science) gave an incredulous gasp. 'Free periods! 4C? God, man, they'd tear the school to pieces.'

There was a considerable hubbub of mixed reactions, and the Headmaster, who couldn't see what common rooms had to do with *education*, was relieved to see that it was time for afternoon school. He masterfully appointed a committee, under the chairmanship of Mrs Bryce, to look into the whole matter and to make practical recommendations. After which he swept off to teach 5A about Figures of Speech.

The only person left in the staffroom was Mr Rees-Jones, the inevitable Welsh maths teacher, who kept his class waiting while he took another quick look at the 'Appointments' pages of *The Times Ed. Supp.* 'The air's too hot to breathe round here, boy,' he muttered.

two

Education and Society

STUDENT teachers tend to be much more concerned about acquiring the technical skills of teaching rather than considering their ultimate aims. There is always a demand for more time to be spent on teaching practice and 'curriculum courses', and far less to be spent on the academic study of Philosophy, Psychology and Sociology.

It is difficult not to sympathize with this demand – but only because these subjects are often very badly presented. Books on the 'Philosophy of Education', for example, are often very obstruse simply because their authors are poor teachers. And books on psychology and sociology (with some honourable exceptions) tend to be verbose and dull.

If students are simply *instructed* in these subjects so that they can scrape and pass in their final exams then there is no doubt that their time would be better spent learning their job by trial and error in the classroom.

At least they might become efficient *teachers* in this way, though their roles as *educators* would be limited. (There is nothing about the word 'teacher' to suggest that his accomplishment is worth while – one can *teach* useless subjects – whereas built into the concept of 'educator' is the notion that what is taught is worth while.)

In this chapter I shall try to show why it is of vital importance for students to develop a clear concept of their aims, and why this involves some capacity for philosophical thinking.

It is apparent from Chapter One that there is bound to be a

close connection between the values of a particular society and the curricula of its schools; for the schools are preparing their pupils to take a place in that society, and they must teach subjects which are *valued* in that society by methods which are *approved* of in that society.

If a society were static and isolated, if its technology, culture, religion, population and political structure remained constant, it would not be necessary for teachers to give much thought to the aims of education. They might devise more efficient teaching methods, but they would go on teaching more or less the same things for the same motives.

There are still a number of such societies in existence, where the education of the young has remained the same for centuries: but inevitably they will eventually have to come to terms with the outside world – often with spectacular suddenness. For example, in 1930 the fishing village of Manus (described by Margaret Mead in *Growing up in New Guinea*) was a static society of the sort defined above. But in the Second World War it became an American naval base, and encountered modern technology for the first time: life could not be the same again. Now the island is struggling to develop a new way of life – and a new form of education for the young. Teachers will have to define their aims extremely carefully: they will want to transmit the culture of the past, but they must prepare the children, vocationally and culturally, for an entirely different world. Whose values are they to adopt?

In a less spectacular way the same thing is happening *continuously* in nearly all societies; for they have developing technologies, their population is increasing, their contacts with other societies are becoming more involved, religious beliefs are changing, and moral values are inevitably in a constant state of flux.

All this means that educational aims cannot remain static. Unthinking teachers *cannot* do their job adequately.

At the most obvious level, there must be changes in the body of factual knowledge transmitted to pupils. It is no use teaching only fishing, boat building and navigation if one's pupils are going to be engineers. It is foolish to devote half the available time to Latin and Greek if one's pupils are going to be scientists and business-men (yet it took generations for our Public Schools to adapt to social changes consequent to the Industrial Revolution). It is pointless to concentrate on Euclidian geometry when other math-ematical thinking has been shown to be more useful, or Clause Analysis if this can be shown to have no value in the study of modern English usage. Unthinking teachers will go on doing the job they were trained to do – even if there is no longer any point in it.

But the question of what *body of information* is passed on can be largely determined by teacher-training. Provided that teachers are trained to churn out the new stuff rather than the old, edu-cation, in this sense, need never be more than forty years or so out of date. And what teachers are trained to churn out can be de-cided by a comparatively small number of thinking education-alists.

Much more critical is the way in which teachers influence the social and moral attitudes of their pupils. In a society changing as rapidly as ours the teacher needs to re-evaluate his influence con-tinuously.

As one example, consider the fairly recent effects of (*a*) popu-lation increase, (*b*) earlier physical maturity, (*c*) extended period of formal education, and (*d*) the development of contraception – all in relation to our sexual mores.

'Officially' (and often hypocritically), there is still an attitude that sex in marriage is good and that sex before or outside mar-riage is bad. 'Unofficially' the general attitude is that the *quality* of sexual relationships is what matters and that individuals should be free to decide on their sexual conduct for themselves provided that the feelings and needs of others are fully respected.

But on this subject most teachers are still way behind the times. Whatever they may think themselves, and however they may *behave*, they transmit the 'official' attitude to increasingly scepti-cal pupils – who reject it without developing anything positive in its place.

In human terms it is not of such critical importance that teachers tend to be out of date on *factual* matters, but when they are influencing social and moral attitudes they are affecting the very quality of human life – and this is of the highest significance.

How society and education interacted in the past, and how education differs from one type of society to another, are respectively the concern of *educational history* and *comparative education*. Reading in both these fields is suggested in the bibliography at the end of this book, and I would be venturing outside my field to say any more about them here.

But instead of having a look at real educational systems perhaps it would be helpful if this chapter concluded with some purely hypothetical situations in which particular aspects of a society are bound to affect the educational aims.

1. Imagine a primitive agricultural society which is constituted of 70 per cent slaves and 30 per cent ruling class. The religion of the society stresses the ephemeral and unpleasant nature of human life, and conceives of a heaven in which the ruling classes will spend their eternal after-life in a state of bliss – especially if they pass on to heaven while at the peak of physical health. The religion therefore demands the ritual sacrifice, at the age of 17, of all the ruling population except (*a*) those destined by birth to become priests, and (*b*) the daughters of priests whose role is to have a large number of children by a succession of condemned 17-year-olds. (Such a society, especially if geographically isolated, is logically possible. It would not be likely to survive very long in this form, but that need not concern us here.)

With regard to education in this society, there are three distinct features to bear in mind.

Firstly, *religion*. How might the education of the young ruling class be affected by the doctrine that life on earth is simply a brief preparation for eternity? Since they have no career to prepare for, what is it necessary for them to learn? Assuming they attended schools, what sort of curriculum would be appropriate, beyond religious instruction and sport?

Secondly, *class*. Those destined to become priests or mothers will obviously require a more extensive education. Presumably the priests will need to exercise power over the slaves, and this is likely to be based on religious fear and on some apparently magical knowledge of agriculture. What sort of curriculum would the trainee priests need?

The slaves do not expect an after-life because they do not believe they have souls – life on earth is all they have. The only education they will be allowed will be minimal. What would it consist of?

Thirdly, *sex status*. When men and women have a different status in society this is another form of class distinction. It is assumed that all the priests are men, and that all the power lies in their hands. Will the education of *all* ruling class girls be different from that of the youths? What sort of curriculum will be needed for the child bearers – who will have large numbers of children but no husbands?

As with any class system, political power lies in the hands of a minority. Why is *indoctrination* (rather than education) necessary if the society is to preserve its existing structure? Why would real education for the slaves be undesirable in the eyes of the priests?

2. The ultimate values of the last society lay in a prospective after-life offering eternal happiness. By contrast, the ultimate values in Aldous Huxley's *Brave New World* concern earthly pleasure. The aim of education in this society is 'to promote self-indulgence up to the very limits imposed by hygiene and economics'. For if people can indulge all their desires they will be content, for the most part, with the prevailing order – social stability will be achieved and there will be no threat (in the form of war or revolution or poverty) to the pursuit of pleasure.

But if people's desires are to be satisfied then those desires must be manipulated by 'education' so that their satisfaction is physically possible. Thus babies in *Brave New World* are moulded by

conditioning and indoctrination into five grades of human being –
from the Alphas who do the work involving high intelligence, to
the 'mass-produced' Epsilons who do work involving mindless
routine. Everyone is happy in his work; the 'slaves' are not forced
to serve the others by physical force. The Epsilons have been
conditioned to dislike the idea of brain work: they prefer simple
routine and short working hours, whereas the Alphas have been
conditioned to enjoy responsibility. 'Education' in the Brave New
World consists, therefore, partly in producing people who have
predictable desires which society can satisfy. This contrasts very
directly, of course, with the Victorian stress on educating people to
control their natural desires by exercising self-discipline and re-
straint.

Anyone who has read *Brave New World* will know how
thoroughly Huxley worked out the implications of the basic concept – and what he has to say about education perfectly demon-
strates the theme of this chapter as the following quotation
indicates:

A student asks the Director why it is necessary to condition lower
caste children to hate flowers.

Patiently the D.H.C. explained. If the children were made to
scream at the sight of a rose, that was on grounds of high economic
policy. Not so very long ago (a century or thereabouts), Gammas,
Deltas, even Epsilons, had been conditioned to like flowers – flowers
in particular and wild nature in general. The idea was to make them
want to be going out into the country at every available opportunity,
and so compel them to consume transport.

'And didn't they consume transport?' asked the student.

'Quite a lot,' the D.H.C. replied. 'But nothing else.'

Primroses and landscapes, he pointed out, have one grave defect:
they are gratuitous. A love of nature keeps no factories busy. It was
decided to abolish the love of nature, at any rate among the lower
classes; to abolish the love of nature, but *not* the tendency to consume transport. For of course it was essential that they should keep
on going to the country, even though they hated it. The problem was
to find an economically sounder reason for consuming transport than
a mere affection for primroses and landscapes. It was duly found.

'We condition the masses to hate the country,' concluded the Director. 'But simultaneously we condition them to love all country sports. At the same time, we see to it that all country sports shall entail the use of elaborate apparatus. So that they consume manufactured articles as well as transport. Hence those electric shocks.'*

'I see,' said the student, and was silent, lost in admiration?

3. Finally, imagine a European society whose ultimate values lay in achieving wealth, power, and status, and whose major sins were 'lack of moral fibre', effeminacy, non-productivity, and non-conformity.

In such a society what might be the attitude of right-wing politicians towards:

(*a*) 'learning through play' in primary schools;
(*b*) liberal studies for science students;
(*c*) raising the school-leaving age;
(*d*) corporal punishment in schools;
(*e*) deferring specialization until *after* the first year at university or college.

* Electric shocks had been used to condition lower caste children to hate flowers and books.

.

three

The Curriculum

MOST readers will have experienced, in their secondary schools, a 'subject-centred' curriculum. In fact, some people may be surprised to realize that there can, in principle, be radically different sorts of curricula.

A subject-centred curriculum reflects the educational philosophy that there are certain fields of knowledge worth studying, that teachers and examining bodies are the right people to decide what these fields should be, and that what is worth teaching falls most conveniently under adult-conceived headings such as Mathematics, Geography, Domestic Science and so on. It also tends to be part of the philosophy that each of these subjects should be taught by an orderly process which begins with very simple concepts and develops more complex ones.

Another sort of educational philosophy is reflected by 'child-centred' education, which is currently very much in favour in progressive primary schools. According to this we should not start by teaching mainly under subject headings because 'subjects' are an artificial, adult invention; it is best if the children discover *for themselves* that there are different sorts of knowledge, and acquire skill in different modes of thought (such as scientific enquiry, mathematics, history) by a process of achieving aims which arise from their own interests. To a lay observer this sort of curriculum could appear haphazard and disorganized, but in fact the order of learning new things is determined more by the pattern of psychological development in each child rather than by the logical structure of different 'subjects'.

Supporters of child-centred education rightly point out that the traditional combination of subjects is not comprehensive enough to cater for all educational needs, and that 'subject-teaching' tends to lead to pupils acquiring a range of *facts* in a particular field rather that an understanding of *principles*. What matters in child-centred education is not that pupils should acquire neat bundles of facts but that they should develop the various capacities for acquiring knowledge for themselves. Instead of being passive receptacles for knowledge supplied by teachers, pupils are seen as active self-educators: the role of the teacher ceases to be that of a disseminator of facts and becomes that of a counsellor.

So far, I have deliberately depicted subject-centred education and child-centred education as though they are incompatible with each other (as indeed many teachers believe). But in fact both concepts are too woolly to be necessarily contradictory: one can, of course, have a subject-based curriculum without committing all the abominations feared by its critics. Any good subject teacher will be more concerned with encouraging pupils to think and learn for themselves than with instructing them in a certain number of facts.

Nevertheless it is perhaps true that a subject-based curriculum, combined with the demands of subject-based examinations, does in fact encourage cramming, especially in secondary schools. But a greater danger is that if the various subject syllabuses are planned independently, pupils will fail to see the cross-connections which exist because the same form of thought can be equally valuable in different 'subjects'. They will not, for example, apply *scientific* thinking to what they learn in *geography*.

Good schools try to create as many cross-connections as possible by planning the curriculum as a whole. For example, principles of design learned in Art can be used in Metalwork if pupils manufacture articles that they have designed themselves; knowledge of history, art, economics and literature could all be related to the study of a particular area of the world; English and 'modern' maths can join forces in a study of logic.

Some schools (both primary and secondary) favour the *project* method of inter-relating subjects, sometimes using a system of team teaching. All the pupils in one year (or a 'family' group selected from different years) might study a theme (which could be The Sea, Pollution, Energy and so on) and the teachers join forces to show what contribution their special knowledge can make. The project method is in principle a useful way of patching up some of the defects of subject-centred education, through in practice it often fails because the teachers lack the imagination to relate successfully or because the planners have no clear idea of what they are trying to achieve. No educational magic is achieved simply by getting pupils to paint pictures of the sea in Art, write poems about the sea in English, study ocean currents in Geography, read the Kon-Tiki Expedition in History, and pretend to be a tidal wave in Drama. In fact the children would just get sea-sick.

But at its best the project method can genuinely demonstrate that the solving of practical problems (such as air-pollution) requires a range of different sorts of knowledge and skills.

Another way of improving a subject-based curriculum is to have a 'core' subject, such as English, which is programmed in such a way that the work done in English can be followed up simultaneously in every other subject. Two textbooks which I wrote with Jack Cross (*The Language of Ideas*, 1 and 2, Hutchinson Educational) provided the basis for one sort of curriculum with English as the core subject, but such a programme is only possible if the school sets its own examinations. Mode 3 C.S.E., an examination set by an individual school on the basis of its own syllabus, enables this sort of approach in the final stages of secondary education; but unfortunately pupils working for external examinations are forced to follow syllabuses which were conceived as separate units.

Yet another kind of curriculum might be described as 'state-centred'. Here the ultimate aim of the educators is to prepare pupils to live according to certain political ideals. As Kalenin, a former president of the Soviet Union, put it:

Communist principles, taken in their elementary form, are the principles of highly educated, honest, advanced people; they are love for one's socialist motherland, friendship, humanity, honesty,

love for socialist labour, and a great many other universally understood qualities. The nurturing, the cultivation of these attributes,
of these lofty qualities, is the most important part of communist
education.

There are many other ways of classifying theories about curriculum. One of them, 'life-centred' education, is the subject of
the next two chapters. But rather than describe more of these
theories it is more important for the purposes of this book to investigate what factors *should* influence teachers in deciding what sort
of curriculum to adopt. And three of the most important of these
factors are:

(*a*) current ideals (social, moral, political and religious)
(*b*) current notions about child psychology, and
(*c*) the nature of knowledge itself.

CURRENT IDEALS

We have already seen how theories about education are bound to
be powerfully influenced by ideals. Plato's *Republic* gives a very
full account of the sort of education that he thought would produce the rulers for his ideal society, and in the *Laws* he describes
an appropriate education for the lower orders. Another very
different sort of utopia is depicted in Aldous Huxley's *Island*,
where he imagines a society which combines the best features of
Western materialism with those of Eastern spiritualism. His description of education in a Utopian school is of considerable
interest in this context. And to take one example from the real
world, the quotation from Kalenin reminds us that the Russian
brand of communism has a very direct influence on what is taught
in schools. For example, religious education is banned, and subjects as diverse as history, psychology, agriculture and anthropology have been presented in ways thought to be consistent with
Marxian theory.

CURRENT NOTIONS OF CHILD PSYCHOLOGY

But equally important in practice is the sort of picture that adults have of the child's mind. If, for example, one believed that at birth the mind is a *tabula rasa*, a blank sheet of paper to be written on, as it were, by experience, and if one regarded the child's personality as something that could be moulded into any shape by education, then perhaps one would incline towards authoritarian modes of education in primary schools, and towards a subject-based curriculum. If you believed that children were born in a state of sin from which they can only be redeemed by a strict and pious upbringing, your views on education would be radically different from those of Rousseau, who held the 'noble savage' concept of mankind and believed that 'God makes all things good; man meddles with them and they become evil'.

Many important educational theories in the past have reflected a particular view of child psychology. Readers will find references later in this book to the work of Pestalozzi, Herbart, Froebel, Dewey and Montessori, all of whom founded their practical ideas of teaching on hypotheses about how children learn.

And in a vaguer kind of way different popular attitudes towards children have each dominated certain eras and had a considerable influence on education. In Victorian times there was a curious ambivalence: children were nasty, noisy things to be suppressed and redeemed, but at the same time they were endowed with a sickly innocence which was purely an adult invention. On this issue it is illuminating to compare Victorian writings for children (such as that reproduced in *The Flowers Of Delight,* de Vries, Dobson) with the best of modern children's literature (such as the novels of Alan Garner). It is also very interesting to study how children are depicted in literature at different periods; it is only during this century that writers have taken them seriously and made them recognizably human. This ties in with the fact that the *study* of children's behaviour is a comparatively recent innovation. Most of the educational theorists prior to this century had preconceived notions about children, and it never occurred to test these notions by scientific methods of observation and experiment.

As was to be expected, the development of appropriate forms of scientific enquiry has given us a radically new understanding of the educational needs of children, and since satisfactory personal relationships seem to be a prerequisite of satisfactory learning, such knowledge is obviously of great importance to all parents and teachers.

From analysts like Melanie Klein and John Bowlby we have learned a great deal about the emotional growth of children; and this knowledge is relevant to the *curriculum* in a variety of ways, some of which are indicated in the next chapter. From psychologists like Piaget and Erikson we are learning about the ways in which children form different sorts of concepts and the developmental stages through which children pass. Piaget, for example, suggests that there are five phases of growth which in terms of development goals are:

(1) The co-ordination of sensory and motor impressions, the exploration of 'self' as a frame of reference.
(2) The exploration of the environment, the discovery of the relation between 'self' and 'non-self'.
(3) The mastery of symbols with which to describe the world.
(4) The beginnings of understanding the workings of the world without, however, understanding the general principles which underly them.
(5) The grasp of logical and abstract principles.

Each new phase tends to occur roughly at the same sort of age in nearly all children, and this clearly ought to influence what teachers do with certain age groups. To take the most obvious example it is no good making children in phase 4 learn abstract principles which they do not *understand*: it is more appropriate to provide them with suitable facilities for exploring, for discovering the facts which will later become the raw material of principle-formation. And each child develops along different conceptual fronts at different speeds, so that the teacher should not rely on a curriculum which presupposes an even rate of development of different mental skills in the individual child (let alone of all the children in a class).

Other psychologists have made specific studies of how children learn to read, how they form number concepts, how they learn to generalize, and so on: such knowledge is clearly of relevance to the organization of the curriculum as well as to teaching methods as such.

THE NATURE OF KNOWLEDGE

The actual structure of the traditional school curriculum (with its selection of subjects like maths, geography, English and so on) is largely the result of historical accidents. Very little thought has been given to how the structure can *best* serve its purpose in 'the education of the whole man' except in so far as there have been attempts to provide a 'balanced' education by seeing that everyone does some 'Arts' and some 'Science' in the lower stages of secondary education. Yet the growing tendency to place importance on 'general studies' in sixth forms, and to defer specialization in universities, indicates that there is widespread dissatisfaction with the traditional curriculum. In secondary schools there is much talk of 'cross-fertilization' and in primary schools of 'integration': teachers are aware that a lot of important learning is slipping through the gaps between 'subjects' and that the 'subjects' themselves are not always serving their intended function in the educational process as a whole.

Part of the trouble has been caused by a failure to distinguish between what Professor Hirst* calls *forms* of thought and *fields* of knowledge. A form of thought is one which has clearly defined criteria by which it is properly conducted: there will be appropriate ways of discovering new information, and appropriate methods for assessing the truth of assertions. *Mathematics* is a

* *Philosophical Analysis and Education*, ed. Archambault, Routledge & Kegan Paul.

clear example of a form of thought, for here the methods involve deduction from a set of axioms, and there are clear rules concerning the methodology of deduction. Mathematical thinking is quite different from that involved in the *physical sciences*, where observation, hypothesis and experiment can be conducted along reasonable lines to reach accurate conclusions. *History* is distinct from both mathematics and science in the ways used to support arguments and reach conclusions, and this again is distinct from the forms of thought involved where one makes assertions about the values of works of *art*. Professor Hirst also gives *moral thinking* as an example of a form of thought, since the kind of evidence one would give for saying 'It is wrong to break a promise' seems to contain elements different from those in, say, 'historical' evidence.

A *field* of thought is one in which a number of forms of thought are necessary. For example, *geography* involves scientific thinking (e.g. in meteorology, oceanography, etc.), historical thinking (with regard to anthropology, evolution, political geography, etc.) and mathematical thinking (climate, population, economics, etc.). Other examples of fields of knowledge include engineering, politics and familiar school subjects such as English, Domestic Science and Current Affairs. But there can be an infinite number of fields of knowledge, whereas there are comparatively few well defined *forms*.

All the knowledge that Man possesses has been achieved through exercising the various forms of thought, and for a person to be educated 'as a whole man' it seems logically necessary that he should be initiated, at some stage, into every form of thought which has its own discipline. Eventually, of course, he will have to specialize. He may become a pure mathematician, or gain special knowledge of a field such as engineering. But if his choice is to be a free one it is essential that he reaches it from the strength of a genuinely liberal education (and this statement is a tautology if we accept Professor Hirst's definition of 'liberal education'*).

It seems, therefore, that the curriculum should be so designed as
* *op. cit.*

to initiate pupils into the various forms of thought. They are not simply to be taught the rules: they must become *practitioners* of the forms – for nothing useful can be learned about, say, mathematical thinking unless one actually *does* it. It is not particularly significant what *fields* occur on the timetable until the question of 'vocational education' arises; for pupils who can *think* in a variety of ways will be equipped to extend their knowledge and abilities in any field which interests them.

We now come to purely practical problems about how the curriculum can best be designed to fulfil its purpose. We must not suppose that there is any *a priori* reason for starting with forms and then combining them into fields, or for starting with fields and then helping pupils to understand the forms which are involved in them. It does not, in fact, very much matter which of these courses we take provided that the teachers are clear about what they are trying to achieve. If they were not, it would be easy to teach, say, geography as a body of facts; and if the subject is taught in this way the pupils may well get nothing of educational value from it.

But having said that the priority is good teaching of how to think in a variety of ways, we need to consider if there is anything sacred about the traditional combination of school subjects: is this combination, in practice, one which provides maximum opportunity for pupils to learn to *think*? Should the curriculum include Latin and Chemistry, but not Philosophy or Psychology? Which fields of science can provide the best grounding in scientific method – physics? botany? astronomy? On what basis should such a choice be made? If pupils can pursue a limited number of Arts subjects, which of these is the most important in helping pupils to develop a basis for aesthetic judgement? And also there are many questions about teaching *methods*. How can disciplines most effectively be taught? If one has a subject-based curriculum, how can teachers co-operate so that the curriculum is 'integrated'?

To summarize, we have seen that the curriculum should be related to our social ideals, that it must take into account all that is known about child psychology, and that it must cater for the development of a wide range of forms of thought. There can never be any final answers to how all this can be achieved most effectively; but in the next two chapters I shall take the plunge and describe two existing sorts of curricula in primary and secondary schools which seem to me to reflect the best of modern educational practice.

I would have liked to say much more about 'forms of thought' but perhaps readers could learn more by discussing with experts such questions as: What is 'historical thinking'? What criteria are there for justifying the statement that the main causes of the first world war were a, b, and c? What is 'moral thinking'? How can one justify one's moral beliefs? What rules govern 'scientific thinking'? How can one justify one's belief in God? – and so on.

four

Process Education

A CERTAIN primary school had no formal groupings of its pupils, no timetable and no subject syllabuses. When the school day started pupils continued half-finished projects or began new ones. The projects arose naturally from the children's own interests, and were pursued either individually or in groups which were formed spontaneously by the children themselves (because a particular starting point happened to appeal to them). Such a group might contain children ranging in age from 7 to 11. During the course of, say, a month, the sort of work involved in the projects could be analysed and shown to contain nearly all the ingredients that might be taught separately in a 'formal' school *and*, of course, many ingredients that might not be found in any other sort of curriculum.

For example, a particular child happened to notice that the main entrance to the local church was a comparatively new part of the building. On the opposite side of the church, facing away from the village, was the original main entrance, now sealed off. The child asked the teacher why the church used to face 'the wrong way', and a discussion arose in which one 8-year-old suggested that perhaps when the church was first built it faced a village which no longer existed.

The teacher asked how they could find out if this was the case, and this was the beginning of a project largely organized by the 8-year-old with a group of six older children. They discovered when the church was built and established that it was older than nearly all the buildings in the existing village. From local records and from reference books they discovered that the original village had indeed been on the other side of the church. They obtained permission from local farmers to conduct an archaeological dig, mapped the original site and discovered a variety of tools, pottery and so on, which they attempted to date by using reference books. Ultimately the collection was passed on to a local museum. (Meanwhile some of the other groups of children were experimenting with differently shaped kites, composing a piece of music for simple instruments that they had made themselves, investigating the sort of plant life existing at different levels of a pond and testing the accuracy of a variety of primitive clocks which again they had made themselves.)

It hardly needs spelling out that the archaeological project involved nearly every 'subject' in an ordinary curriculum, though the obvious elements are history, geography, R.E., Maths and English. And the project as a whole is a very good example of scientific method – an hypothesis was tested by a variety of experiments and found to be correct.

The children were enthusiastic because they virtually conceived the project themselves, and because they were able to take it as far as they wanted to go and then go on to something different. In fact at this particular school (which admittedly had unusually dedicated teachers) not only were all pupils totally absorbed in their work for the bulk of the school day but also tended to disregard 'play time' and 'home time', and were often found at work as early at 8 a.m. and as late as 6 p.m.

Formal teaching existed only in the sense that a particular group might get stuck with a problem, for example, through not knowing particular mathematical principles, and the teacher, noticing this, would instruct them as far as possible. Incidentally, the success of the school in the '11-plus' markedly increased each year that the school was run in this way.

Whatever the virtues and defects of this system may be (these will be discussed later), many educationists would describe it as 'integrated'. In current jargon they might say that the school had 'an integrated curriculum', or that the Head clearly 'believed in integration'. In other contexts one hears of 'the integrated day', an expression which is sometimes used to mean 'a day during which work is organized as a whole and not broken up into lessons on different topics'.

The word 'integration' means so many different things to different people that I am at loss to provide a useful definition. In fact, to some people, 'integration' seems to be the name of some sort of religion rather than a name for specific educational methods.

An integrated curriculum *could* mean one worked out as a whole so that pupils were able to see cross-connections between different subjects, and an integrated day *could* mean a day in which different subject teachers all contributed to the study of one topic. On the other hand, some people use the word 'integration' because they believe in a woolly kind of way that 'knowledge is a whole' and 'should be taught as a whole' – but apart from the fact that this does not mean anything very clear one *could* believe that the best way for pupils to acquire the 'whole' is to make a systematic study of various *parts* of the whole. But this would not satisfy the more mystical integrationists. 'Integration is not "made" by "assembling" two subjects,' writes V. Lowenfield; 'integration happens from within.' And in the Plowden Report we find:

> 'Integration is not only a question of allowing time for interests which do not fit under subject headings; it is as much a matter of seeing the different dimensions of subject work and of using forms of observation and communication which are most suitable to a given sequence of learning.'

– a passage which I find almost totally obscure.

In the school that I described I am not sure which of these interpretations (if any) would have satisfied the headmaster. In so far as the school was successful educationally one might draw up a whole list of relevant features, only some of which are obviously to do with integration in any shape or form.

(1) The staff worked as a team, and they worked *with* the pupils. Their roles were not differentiated.

(2) The children formed their own groups.
(3) Every school day was integrated in the sense that it was not broken up into lessons on different topics.
(4) Knowledge was not presented to the pupils in pre-packaged units.
(5) No attempt was made to impose adult methods of problem-solving. Often pupils (and teachers) discovered methods quite new to them.
(6) All the work arose from starting-points suggested by the pupils, and therefore in principle the pupils were able to develop ideas which would never have arisen in a subject-based curriculum.
(7) The pupils had much more responsibility than usual for the conduct of their work. Inevitably, they often worked unsupervised both in and out of the school buildings.

But if one chose to point to a school which works in this way and say, '*That* is integration', it is not at all easy to see what special magic lies in the word which enables it to encompass so many different qualities.

My own feeling is that the seven qualities *do* cohere in some special sort of way which represents the best sort of education in primary schools, but that the concept of integration is not helpful to understanding *why* they cohere. However, before going on to introduce what I think is a more useful concept it is necessary to throw in a word of warning. I have no *evidence* at all for believing that primary schools function best in this way: there is such a deplorable lack of research in education that it will be many years before satisfactory evidence, one way or the other, is available. Concerning the school that I described, for example, there has been no follow-up to see how well the pupils succeeded in their secondary education. In any case, it is notoriously difficult to discover whether new approaches in education work because they are theoretically sound or whether the most important factor is the enthusiasm of convinced teachers. Certainly the school I described could be an utter failure if the same methods were used by teachers who neither understood what they were doing nor possessed the instinctive skills of that particular headteacher.

Having issued this warning I would like to make a new start suggested in the first place by a now old-fashioned psychological definition:

> *Integration*: co-ordination and relation of the total processes of perception, interpretation and reaction ensuring a normal, effective life.

If one asks 'In integrated education *what* is it that is integrated?' the answer is not (in this sense) the curriculum, or the day, or knowledge: rather one would reply: 'Teachers should help their pupils to develop as "whole" or "integrated" people.'

Of course, 'educating the whole man' is an old battle-cry, but not one to be despised on that account. Traditionally it has meant something like 'educating the body, mind and spirit', and has been contrasted with education which develops the intellect but not the emotions, which favours book-learning but not 'learning through experience', which caters for the welfare of the mind but not of the soul, or which prepares people to accept a given role in society but never to rebel against the expectations of society.

The 'whole man' concept, however, is much more helpful if considered in modern psychological terms. I could not even begin to give a satisfactory account here, but as a conceptual starting point I would like to introduce the terms 'primary' and 'secondary' mental processes. These are two types of mental functioning, the former being characteristic of *unconscious* mental activity, the latter being characteristic of *conscious* thinking.*

Primary processes (exemplified in dreaming and fantasy) ignore space and time and find expression through symbols which may or may not be comprehensible to the conscious mind. The main function of the primary processes (in lay terms) is to help us to alleviate tensions of which we may not be conscious, tensions caused by the

---

* It is only fair to remind the reader at this point that some psychologists, such as Eysenck, are antagonistic to the concept of 'the unconscious' and would dismiss most of this chapter as being metaphysical nonsense.

sheer impossibility of satisfying all our instinctual desires. Dreams, for example, seem to function by resolving internal conflicts via a special sort of symbolic 'language'. However much sleep people get they are liable to become unreasonably angry and to suffer from acute anxiety if they are awakened each time they begin to dream. Such experiments have been conducted with volunteers who are thought to be dreaming because of mental activity detected on an electroencephalograph, and the effects on the emotional state of the volunteers were much more pronounced than those caused by random interruption of sleep. Freud believed that people dream so that they can stay asleep, but recent work suggests that it is more appropriate to think that people sleep in order to dream.

Secondary processes are logical, conscious and related to reality. They are processes we can *use* and *control*.

Primary and secondary processes overlap, as in day-dreaming and in any form of imaginative and creative activity. One can be conscious that one *is* day-dreaming, yet the form such activity takes is partly determined by unconscious desires and tensions. A poet thinks in an orderly and rational way when constructing a poem; but he is also, as it were, tapping the reservoir of his unconscious mind, and using images and words which have many unconscious associations beneath their literal meaning. All art is enriched in this way, and is endowed with qualities which can communicate directly with the deeper levels of the observer's personality long before the work is 'understood' at a conscious level.

With this in mind consider the following poem by Robert Graves.

THE COOL WEB

Children are dumb to say how hot the day is,
How hot the scent is of the summer rose,
How dreadful the black wastes of the evening sky,
How dreadful the tall soldiers drumming by.

But we have speech, to chill the angry day,
And speech, to dull the rose's cruel scent
We spell away the overhanging night,
We spell away the soldiers and the fright.

There's a cool web of language winds us in,
Retreat from too much joy or too much fear:
We grow sea-green at last and coldly die
In brininess and volubility.

But if we let our tongues lose self-possession,
Throwing off language and its watery clasp
Before our death, instead of when death comes,
Facing the wide glare of the children's day,
Facing the rose, the dark sky and the drums
We shall go mad no doubt and die that way.

At a conscious level this poem 'works' by making the point (very relevant to this chapter) that adults are free from many childhood terrors because they can 'explain them away' – *language* (for which we could substitute secondary thought processes) gives them the power to understand phenomena which then cease to be frightening. If adults had to endure the intensity of children's emotions they would go mad.

But the poem works at an unconscious level as well. Why did Graves choose those particular examples (the cruel scent of the rose, the drumming soldiers) rather than a million other possible examples?

However, I did not quote this poem as an object for literary criticism. Rather, I want to use it as a starting point for a consideration of what it is *like* to be a small child.

At first babies are, in a sense, omnipotent. They cry for food and food appears. They cry because they are uncomfortable and they are made comfortable. But this magical state of affairs is short-lived. The baby's desires grow more differentiated and are not always satisfied. Bit by bit boundaries are laid down: the differences between 'self' and 'not self' are defined. At three months the baby examines the movements of his hands at varying distances from his eyes. He brings objects to his mouth for examination, and he may literally reach for the moon. Gradually he differentiates people as well as objects and during the second half of his first year he enters what Winnicott calls the 'stage of concern', that stage of development at which the baby gradually becomes able to form percepts of the movements, needs and feelings of a being separate from himself (normally, in the first place, in relation to his mother).

A child of nine months is capable of despair if left outside a shop by his mother. At this stage he has formed a concept of her as a person whose movements he is not able to control, and he is still continuously in need of the 'good enough mothering' described by Winnicott.

According to modern psycho-analytical theory there should be a stable one-to-one relationship consistently (though not continuously) available throughout early babyhood and the first five or six years of life. In the context of this relationship a stable *ego* develops and among its properties are the ability to take part in further relationships and also to be alone without anxiety.

Certain analysts (Winnicott, Bowlby, Fairbairn, Guntrip) describe the various defensive procedures which take place in the absence of adequate relationships. In babyhood the most important of these is described as 'ego splitting', a process whereby the ego is said to lose its integrity and therefore to become more vulnerable and less able to communicate either with itself or with the outside world. This defence is accompanied by a difficulty in dealing with the ambivalence (mixed good and bad feelings) which is a normal part of our relationship with the outside world. Thus for the split ego objects are seen as *either* good *or* bad, and the child cannot tolerate any ambivalent feelings *within* himself. This failure in early relationship weakens the capacity of the self to understand and accept its own needs and feelings, reduces its capacity to feel empathy with others or to learn from them. In particular, with relation to the point of this chapter, it leaves the school child out of touch with his primary thought processes, handicapped in his social relationships within the school and less able to develop his secondary thought processes.

If a child is severely handicapped in this way he will find it so difficult to benefit from the ordinary school environment that he may need psychiatric help. But since we have seen that his problems arise from faulty relationships within the family it is unlikely that he is the *only* person in the family who needs such help. The term 'family process' is one which has come into existence for this very reason, for the psychiatrist needs to know quite a lot about how different members of the family interact at all levels of their personality. Often the child's problems can be alleviated if the family can be helped to gain insight into their behaviour towards each other (and therefore into their primary thought processes).

The aspect of development so far stressed has been the child's ego development. He has moved from the stage of omnipotent personality to what Ausubel calls the stage of 'satellite personality'. He is no longer the centre of the universe, but now he derives his status as an individual by identifying with adults. Later he goes through the 'gang phase' when his friends function as an extension of his family, and later still he will achieve 'primary status', when, in the course of adolescence, he becomes emotionally independent of his parents. He will become a person in his own right, choosing *his* way of life, making *his* decisions. This stage of maturity does not, however, involve total rejection of the values of his family – he will become capable of a 'mature dependence' which will enable him to maintain a fruitful relationship with those who have helped him to become an adult.

I have coined the term 'process education' to highlight the teacher's role in helping the primary school child to emerge as a *person*. I am not confusing the role of a teacher with that of a psychologist, nor am I falling into the trap of implying that 'mental health' is the main aim of education. What I *am* suggesting is that, as surely as a baby needs milk to grow, a primary school child needs education to discover who and what he is. The education of a pre-adolescent child should therefore be conceived in these terms.

Now we come to some extremely difficult questions – questions to which as yet there are no sure answers. The role of the educationist is to ask: 'If we accept this picture of child development what *sort* of education is appropriate? What can school teachers *do* to provide what is needed? What subjects should be taught? Should children work formally as a whole class or informally in groups? Does it matter what methods the teacher uses or is the only crucial factor the quality of his relationship with the pupils?'

Since so many variables are involved we can at least simplify matters to a small degree by considering these questions in the context of what is currently *possible*. We cannot, for example, opt for classes of five in the infant school, and classes of fifteen to twenty in the junior school. We cannot base our plans on the expectation that a school staff will remain fairly constant – between 10 per cent and 50 per cent will leave and be replaced each year. (Young women teachers in particular are likely to stay for no more than three years in their first post.) And we cannot rebuild every school to suit our purposes: we have to work as best we can in the existing buildings.

What we can do, however, is to consider a factor that *can* be comparatively stable; and that is the educational policy of a particular school. If we have good reasons for supposing that one sort of policy is more effective than another we can do our best to encourage other schools to follow suit.

Earlier in the chapter I listed seven features which seemed relevant to the success of an 'integrated' junior school. I said that they seemed to cohere in a special sort of way and that the concept of 'process education' might be helpful in understanding why this should be the case. Unfortunately there is no way I could possibly *prove* that such a coherence exists: all I can do is to ask a number of questions (most of them unanswerable) and leave it to the reader to draw his own conclusion.

D

1. Given that a sound teacher/pupil relationship is a vital factor in education, are there any ways of organizing a school which are likely to *foster* good relationships? Should we avoid a dictatorial, lecturer/audience relationship? How can we encourage teachers to work *with* pupils, so that they learn *from* the pupils as well as teaching them? Can we minimize the bad effects of large classes by getting the children to work in small groups? To what extent is it good for teacher/pupil relationships that pupils should have a degree of freedom in choosing their starting points and developing their interests? Is it important that an atmosphere is created in which it is quite natural for teachers and pupils to work together outside school hours and away from the school buildings? Does it help teacher/pupil relationships if, as far as possible, parents are involved in the work of the school?

While supervising teaching practice I have noticed that it takes about two days for a student to learn all the names of the pupils in his class if they are working in groups on different projects. If the class is arranged formally, with every child doing the same work, it is not uncommon to find that the student takes a week or two to learn all the names. Is this of any significance?

2. Given that children work in groups, how should these groups be formed? Does the teacher know best, working on the idea that groups should be organized according to I.Q., or so that timid children are put with motherly ones, or so that bullies are put with bigger and stronger children? Or is it possible that the children themselves 'know' best, and, apparently haphazardly, fulfil unconscious needs by relating with certain other children? Is it desirable that such groups should remain fixed for long periods, or will children satisfy a greater variety of needs if the groups change according to the project on hand (which in any case will attract certain children at both a primary and secondary level)? In fairly conventional schools it often happens that 'undesirable' groups are formed spontaneously: are there any reasons to suppose that this would be less likely in the sort of school that I have described?

3. If a child wanted to spend project time in designing instruments

of torture, it is quite likely that his unconscious motives would be of interest to a psychiatrist. But most children would opt for less surprising topics such as identifying and assembling the bones of a rabbit. Is it possible that, in pursuing such a topic for conscious, intellectual reasons, the pupil is also fulfilling *unconscious* needs? Perhaps, if children are encouraged to develop work from their own starting points, they are also being helped to stay in touch with their primary thought processes – they are satisfying all levels of their personality.

4. To what extent is *continuity* important, both in preserving 'good enough' relationships with a teacher and in following through a particular project? Given a conventional timetable (with half an hour for Maths, and half an hour for English) is one giving *all* the children in the class the optimum chance of linking their unconscious and conscious educational needs? How can one organize the working day so that these needs are best satisfied?

5. Before we can be preserved from 'too much joy' or 'too much fear' by the tempering influence of secondary thought processes, while we have to face the 'wide glare of the children's day', all of us have to endure inexplicable, intense and often irreconcilable emotions – in adult terms the helplessness of Oedipus hounded by the fates, the jealousy of Othello, the despair of King Lear. Yet such emotions are part of *us*. Children are naturally creative, but notoriously 'dry up' as they grow older. Is this an inevitable consequence of maturing? Or is it the result of an education which traditionally is aimed at developing only the secondary thought processes? How can teachers help pupils to 'stay in touch' with their unconscious minds?

6. Damage to the ego development of a child is almost invariably caused through a failure of communication within the family. If an analogy exists at all, how important is it that *teachers* within a school should work in a way which promotes maximum personal understanding among *themselves*?

*   *   *

If nothing else has emerged from this chapter, I hope that readers will appreciate a little more clearly how little we *know* about primary school education. We are working almost entirely in the dark because of the absence of both coherent educational theory and of 'hard' research. But however vague they may be I hope that the ideas outlined in this chapter will at least indicate areas of educational practice which it is particularly important to investigate.

Interlude 2

By special dispensation, Miss Gifkins was allowed at the end of her probationary year to transfer for one term to Blackmore Junior School. So famous was this establishment for its progressive methods that she felt it was a real privilege to gain a term's experience there.

It was an open-plan school designed by a local architect who had been so carried away by his educational vision that the Local Education Authority had had to plead with him to include any internal walls at all. It was put to him that the head teacher occasionally needed privacy and there was no need for the open-plan concept to embrace the lavatories.

These needs were met, but the building still resembled an aircraft hangar. Teaching in the conventional sense had proved impossible until the staff hit upon the idea of using the dining tables, tipped on their sides during school hours, to form classroom walls – though the word 'classroom' was never used in the presence of Miss Peacock, the head mistress.

'We have no classrooms,' she told Miss Gifkins: 'we have teaching areas. We have no classes: we have Study Groups. We have no streaming: we are Mixed.'

After a tour of the school Miss Gifkins was placed under the supervision of Mr Belfry, who was in charge of Study Group 4B.

'What does "4B" mean?' was Miss Gifkins' first question.

Mr Belfry (who was young enough to be proud of having a young lady under him) tweaked his ginger beard, tugged at the bottoms of the khaki shorts that he had been wearing for Special Activities, and said:

'Bright girl, bright girl. Straight to the point. Well, the "4" means fourth year, and the "B" means yours truly, Belfry. The other fourth year class – I mean, group – is 4A. "A" is for Ansell, that chap just behind the table there, with grass in his hair.'

'How were these groups sorted out? You don't have streaming, I understand.'

'No, certainly not. *Well,* basically we separated the kids into two groups – those who can read well and those who can't. Pointless to have them altogether because you couldn't teach them properly. I've got the group that *can* read. I'm Deputy Head, you see.'

'But this *is* streaming, surely.'

'No, no, no. Mixed ability. Mustn't confuse reading age and I.Q. No, this lot is mixed ability, all right. Look, see that table over there, furthest from the window. Oh hell, the roof's leaking again.'

He gazed round, puzzled. 'Ah, the Bucket Girl is away. Rheumatism. Mmmm. CYNTHIA – you're today's Bucket Girl.'

Cynthia stopped colouring in a duplicated outline of an anonymous fish and placed a bucket under the steady drip of water. Suddenly the source of the drip shifted by about three feet, and she patiently moved underneath.

'They take it in turns, one day each. What was I saying? Oh yes, that group over there. They're the dimmies. Daft as brushes, all of them. Put them near a window and they'd waste their time looking out. Now this table here, these are the Grammar School ones. Great kids.'

Miss Gifkins felt a deep sense of unease.

'How do you use these groups?' she asked. 'Are they all working on different projects?'

'Oh yes, quite different. But we have a Theme for the Week to tie them all together. We call it Integration. Let's start with the dimmies – they're doing a collage.'

The dimmies were engaged in cutting out fish patterns from a printed sheet and sticking them on a sheet of blue sugar paper.

'Couldn't they draw the fish for themselves?' asked Miss Gifkins.

'Well I *suppose* they could, but the drawings wouldn't be as *good*, would they. And they'd take so long over it. You have to give them a sense of achievement, you know.'

They moved to Cynthia's table. 'Quite a different kettle of fish you see. Colouring *in* the patterns. These are much more capable kids – future "A" stream in a sec. mod. Now look at the top lot. Real piece of inspiration, this.'

The top lot were doing long division sums.

'I use assignment cards, you see. Textbooks are so dull and impersonal. That's why I've printed each sum on a cardboard fish. Every time I call out SWIM, they swap fishes.'

The whole school suddenly vibrated with the noise of a hand bell. Miss Peacock strode from Teaching Area to Teaching Area crying 'Barricades down! Barricades down!' as well-drilled children removed the dining tables. She saw Miss Gifkins and seized her by the arm. 'We don't have a school Assembly here,' she said. 'Secular society and all that. We have what you young people would call a Happening. It involves the children so much more you see. Takes them by surprise.'

She stood on a chair and waved for attention.

'This week is Fish week,' she bellowed, 'and I'm going to tell you all a Very Remarkable Story about a certain good, kind man, whose name I *won't* mention, who managed to feed 40,000 people with a few loaves of bread and just a teeny bit of fish. Hands up anyone who . . .'

But by this time Miss Gifkins had fled to a loo, mercifully shielded by one of the precious internal walls; and she smoked a cigarette while the resonance of Miss Peacock's voice relentlessly swung the chain to and fro . . .

five

Thematic Studies

THERE is no reason in principle why the 'process education' of the primary school should not continue beyond the age of 11 at least through the first year of the secondary school. In fact, it has long been recognized that eleven is a very odd age for children to be plunged into quite a different sort of educational environment: it is mainly economic considerations concerning the best use of existing school buildings which have delayed a radical reconstruction of the entire school system.

But by the time children reach the age of 12 or 13 they have normally reached what Piaget calls 'the phase of formal operations'. They become able to *generalize*, to think in terms of abstract *principles*. Piaget gives the following example: a younger child, in 'the phase of concrete operations', would be able to find out that given a certain number of counters arranged in rows one cannot change the *total* number simply by moving the counters from one row to another. A child in the next phase, however, would be able to predict the outcome of this experiment without needing to perform it. He has conceptualized a rule about constancy of quantities.

Once a child is able to generalize from his experience and to think abstractly he will be capable of understanding that mathematics, for example, involves a form of thinking different in *kind* from that required for writing stories or for conducting scientific experiments. He is now ready to learn 'subjects' because he can see why they *are* subjects. The fact that children develop in this way partly accounts for the fact that, generally speaking, primary schools are 'child centred' and secondary schools are 'subject centred'; but the schism is exaggerated by the fact that primary schools anyway tend to attract teachers who like teaching *children*, whereas regrettably secondary schools (especially grammar schools) tend to attract those who prefer the easier task of teaching subjects.

The fact that secondary school children are taught subjects also tends to mean that they will encounter a greater number of teachers. The class teacher in the primary school will usually be in contact with her pupils for at least three quarters of the time, whereas subject teachers in a secondary school will have much less personal contact, perhaps seeing a particular class for less than an hour a week. At the age of 12 or 13 children should be ready intellectually and emotionally to benefit from this state of affairs: they will encounter different points of view and a variety of teaching methods.

But for 'process education' to continue in a form suitable for this stage, for the child to go on developing all levels of his personality, it is not sufficient simply to teach him a selection of academic subjects. Other conditions need to be fulfilled, and I would guess that the most important of them are as follows:

1. Secondary school teachers should be closely in touch with the primary schools from which their pupils come. Otherwise *continuity* is impossible.

2. The pupils still need a 'good enough' relationship with at least one teacher. The school must therefore have a system of pastoral care which will enable him to maintain such a relationship. The organization of the school can do a lot to encourage pastoral care, especially if the timetable is arranged to permit plenty of contact between pupils and their assigned counsellors. And the head teacher can do a lot to encourage this sort of 'quasi-parental relationship' (as Barry Sugarman described it in *An Introduction to Moral Education*, Penguin) by showing that he recognizes its importance and by the extent to which he encourages teacher/pupil contact out of school hours. It is now commonly recognized that

school clubs, sporting activities, camping holidays, expeditions, and so on, can provide the best opportunity for good teacher/ pupil relationships to develop.

3. It is still important that children should be able to work in groups where they can form the sort of human relationships that they most need. It seems likely to me that an unstreamed comprehensive school, with all pupils in mixed ability groups, will provide the best opportunity for this to happen. It is particularly important that boys should go on working with girls: I think it abominable that single-sex schools should ever have existed.

4. It is more important than ever that pupils should be able to exercise responsibility both in their general conduct and in their academic work. Otherwise the development of self-discipline can be crippled.

As far as academic work is concerned it does not in the least surprise me that success in 'A-levels' at formal grammar schools is a very poor predictor of success at university, where self-discipline is essential – for the traditional examination system has imposed such rigid patterns of work that mere cramming has been encouraged.

As for general conduct, it is necessary that there should be rules (as in any community) and that these rules should be strictly enforced. But the rules should always be *reasonable,* genuinely *necessary*, and as *few* as possible in number. It is important that the pupils themselves should be able to exercise some power in deciding what the rules should be: this is part of their education for living responsibly in a democracy.

5. At some stage, the pupil will sense that he needs to specialize, that he cannot pursue the whole range of his interests in any depth, that further self-knowledge can best be achieved by a profounder understanding of selected aspects of the external world. Ideally he will be sufficiently 'in touch' with himself to know what he *needs* to know, and will have maximum freedom of choice. Tragically, most pupils will have left school before this vital stage

is reached, since it will not normally occur until late adolescence. And since we have to recognize that most pupils leave too soon we have to modify secondary school education accordingly, for there are a lot of things that teenagers *must* know before leaving school. Education in secondary modern schools, desite all enlightened attempts to the contrary, tends therefore to degenerate into a sort of crash course in 'practical living'.

Another argument in favour of comprehensive education is that without doubt it encourages more pupils to stay on at school until the age of 18, and in principle can supply a sufficiently wide variety of courses to cater for all individual needs.

6. Lastly, it is important to overcome the many academic disadvantages of a subject-based curriculum. Some methods of doing so were discussed in Chapter Three, but none of them seems to me entirely satisfactory.

The expression 'integrated curriculum' is perhaps more meaningful at this stage than it was in the primary school since we are specifically thinking of ways in which the various subjects can be considered in some sense as a 'whole'. The word 'integrative' might, however, be more precise since 'integrated' suggests a ready-made programme of learning where it is the teachers who have done the *thinking* involved. Perhaps 'integrative' helps to suggest that an active role is demanded of the *pupils*: the curriculum is organized to give pupils the maximum opportunity of seeing for themselves what forms of thought are involved in different fields of knowledge.

The remainder of this chapter is adapted from a paper written by my cousin, the late Dr Roland Harris, when he was deputy head of Woodberry Down Comprehensive School. In this paper he gives his own idea of how the curriculum can be organized in a way which both takes full advantage of subject teaching and at the same time helps each pupil to achieve a coherent understanding of himself in relation to the universe.

THEMATIC STUDIES

The various departments in a comprehensive school, despite good-will and resolutions, find it difficult to put into practical effect any real programme for a unified curriculum. They rely in practice on accidental overlaps, on an alert teacher spotting a possible cross-reference. What we think of as broad education is often little more than a multiplication of disparate subjects.

This multiplication is not only wasteful in itself, but leads to the omission of many aspects of knowledge which perhaps because they are fairly recent in schools have rarely or never been given scope in the traditional curriculum. Such topics are, for example, simple patterns of psychological behaviour whether in the individual or the group observation in younger siblings of, say, reactions to frustration, spoiling, teasing, offers of help; and of the behaviour of gangs of teenagers; and similar material which could lead to mothercraft lessons, or to the better understanding of personality development and national behaviour. Other examples are studies of town planning, of political doctrines, of theories of morality and metaphysics – all things which directly affect the life and behaviour of human beings much more than traditional school learning. It is entirely the fault of the schools if the so-called academic branches of study have become divorced from any practical importance for the pupils; and little can be done to remedy this by a hasty and patched sixth form general studies course. A general course should exist throughout the school; haste and patching would then be unnecessary, and we could hope to have sixth-formers who were full human beings instead of illiterate or innumerate specialists living in the dream world where there is such a monstrosity as the non-vocational subject. All subjects are vocational when they are related to human life.

That this idea has dropped out of educational practice explains, I think, the split between the Science and Arts faculties, rather than does the inherent difficulty or difference between such disciplines. It explains also the general arrogance of the academic specialists towards the crafts, and the contempt of the craft

specialists for the academics. It leads only too readily to the sep-
aratism which the grammar/technical/modern division exempli-
fies, and which the comprehensive school is designed to counteract
– though with little effect if its own curriculum remains essentially
tripartite.

The immediate pedagogic excuse for a reconsideration of these
matters is the problem afforded by providing courses which will
satisfy the type of child who now leaves school at 15, the earliest
statutory age, and in future at 16; but it should be seen that the
same problem applies to the whole school population – particularly, perhaps, to the most intelligent ones.

A curriculum designed to avoid the present disintegration
should be life-centred, rather than child-centred (as in some recent
philosophies of education) or subject-centred (as in the traditional
specialities) or State-centred (as in some present political philosophies of education). Its aim is to interweave subject-knowledge
and self-knowledge, and to enable the pupil to see himself and his
society or social group as part of the total evolutionary process.

A preliminary idea of this may best be shown in the form of a
diagram. (See page 52.)

The responses become of course more and more complex, but
much cross-fertilization will be evident, as, for example, between
hunting and magic, architecture and art, physical and social
sciences, and so on.

One advantage – and danger – of such a scheme is that the
pupils will constantly have to generalize. This mental skill is
seldom trained in present methods of education, being replaced by
the accumulation of facts seldom seen by the pupil to be related to
a direct central theme. The scope of the suggested programme is so
wide that the teacher will need to select very carefully observations
which will have valid extension and so be capable of supporting a
generalization. Few teachers will have the requisite general knowledge to do this, and no textbooks, as yet, exist. It is thus here that
the various departments will have to co-operate most con-
scientiously so that any one teacher may hope to explore the related themes even though these are outside his own speciality.

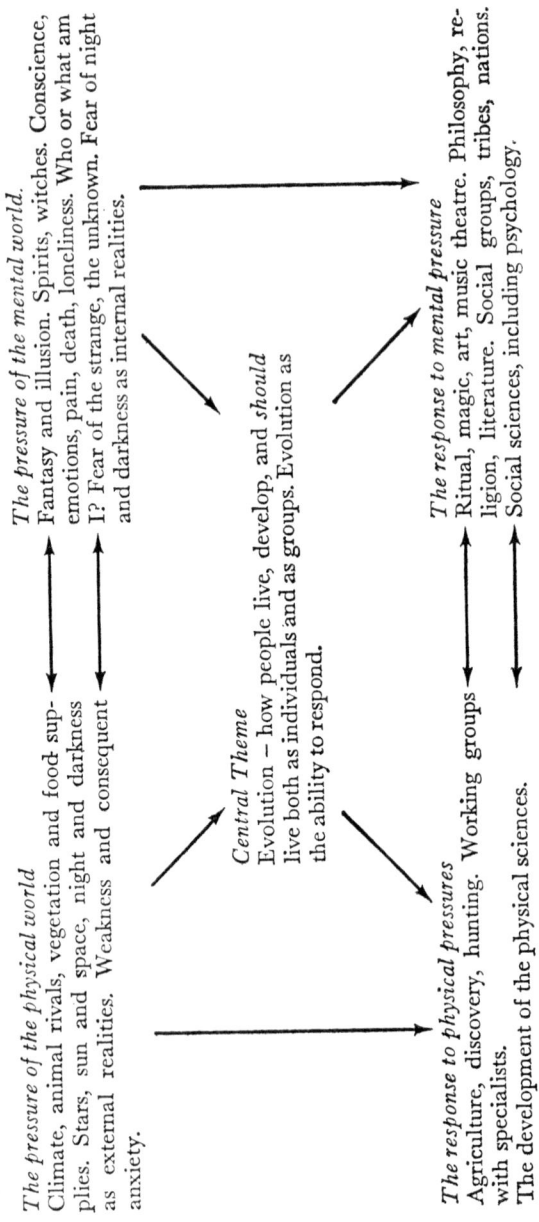

The pressure of the physical world
Climate, animal rivals, vegetation and food supplies. Stars, sun and space, night and darkness as external realities. Weakness and consequent anxiety.

The pressure of the mental world.
Fantasy and illusion. Spirits, witches. Conscience, emotions, pain, death, loneliness. Who or what am I? Fear of the strange, the unknown. Fear of night and darkness as internal realities.

Central Theme
Evolution – how people live, develop, and *should* live both as individuals and as groups. Evolution as the ability to respond.

The response to physical pressures
Agriculture, discovery, hunting. Working groups with specialists.
The development of the physical sciences.

The response to mental pressure
Ritual, magic, art, music theatre. Philosophy, religion, literature. Social groups, tribes, nations. Social sciences, including psychology.

Detailed exploration of specific points would have to be done within a Department, of course. Hence the title of this paper – thematic studies. The themes have to be decided in each year: the syllabus follows. The theme is thus not a *subject*, as in the present system. Nor is it equivalent to the *project* method of study: its aim is to generalize, not to be specific; to map a wide area, not a narrow one. It would, of course, be quite feasible to fit 'projects' into the thematic scheme if they were required.

When children themselves can make sufficient observations, as is most desirable (in, for example, studies of the motivation and reactions of themselves and siblings as individuals, or in field work) the effort to generalize by deduction is of fundamental importance, provided that children are made aware of the limitations of their generalizations: such awareness can lead to good scientific standards of honesty and to a more liberal and tolerant understanding of other people and peoples.

I have not sufficient general knowledge to produce an accurate programme for such a course, but put forward as a tentative indication the following starting point. Where I can, I have indicated which departments are likely to be able to offer help.

The pattern of the course would establish itself as:

(1) Survey of pressure/response systems through history with adequate linking of contributions from all departments. This is the acquisitive and relatively passive part of the course, corresponding roughly to the present 'subject' syllabuses; but often in fact more active both in lending itself easily to various project activities and in feeding the capacity to generalize by links from many departments to the central theme.

(2) Experience of how we do respond – e.g. how we grow as individuals and combine as groups. This is the active and demonstrative part of the course and will necessarily be focused on the present day and the local situation.

It would include such experiences as the following:
how to think: some direct training in logic, deduction, abstraction.

how not to deceive: advertisements, propaganda, charts and statistics, hire purchase, contracts

how to criticize: comparative examples from art, architecture, promise and performance in politics, music, newspapers, drama, etc.

how to be informed: newspapers, reports, TV, paperbacks on, e.g. law, politics, welfare

how to survive: first aid, housecraft, domestic science for both boys and girls

how to mix: etiquette, interviews and discussions, personal relationships, sex education

how to judge: ethics, religion, philosophy.

If we assume that four or five periods a week should go to such a course, two or even three would be likely to be spent on part 2, but of course the experiential work involved would spread back into all the 'subjects' on the timetable and would permeate the entire curriculum. As for part 1, the general theme might be that at first the urgent pressures were external, from nature, animals, illness; but that with time the critical sphere has become internalized, with our own nature (and other men) as the chief source of pressure.

To illustrate what all this would involve in practice I have sketched out what the content of such a course might be in (a) the first year and (b) the final year. Later, readers may be interested in trying to work out what could take place in the middle two or three years of the course.

YEAR ONE

First Term
Central theme: evolution as the ability to respond.

1. The challenge of nature – general introduction showing (perhaps with the use of films and film-strips) the hazards of vol-

canic eruption, hurricane, ice, flood, drought, erosion, fire, predators, the microcosmos and the macrocosmos.

2. The need for response – examples of creatures that failed to
respond. Need for ability to assess external and internal dangers
and problems – we differ from ancient man in that our weakness is
inside ourselves rather than relative to external nature.

The pressures on ancient man: need for food, warmth, shelter,
protection against predators, weakness through isolation and ignorance.
His responses: fire, tools, animal husbandry, beginnings of agriculture, family groups (responses to external pressures); magical art,
ritual, primitive religion (responses to internal pressures).

Departments providing evidence:

science	–	archaeology, zoology, meteorology, physics
art	–	cave paintings
R.E.	–	relationship between magic and religion
technical	–	primitive tools
geography	–	climate, agriculture
history	–	anthropology
English	–	appropriate books (e.g. *The Jungle Book, Lord of the Flies, The Golden Bough*) – how did language begin?

Second Term

Sumerians, Egyptians, Hebrews

The pressures on early civilized man:
Basic food and warmth needs continue (lean years, locusts) and
may even be sharpened by the need to be better organized as tribes
increase and group together in the best geographical locations,
such as the Tigris, Euphrates, Nile.
Danger from own species increases; fears of personal death; loneliness, the power of the unknown.

E

His responses:
Agricultural development – conscious adaptation to local climate; link with astronomy; architecture; weaving; collective cities; functional specialization in armies, priests, etc. Trade, medicine, geometry, pyramids and plural gods, and later Hebrew monotheism; art becomes less magical but functional as symbols of power or as decoration; number; written history; applied psychology – interpretation of dreams; ritual; communal life.

Departments providing evidence: as before, except that Maths and possibly Drama will become more involved.

Third Term

The Greeks

External pressures

Basic needs remain (Odysseus ploughing) but become direct threats in future only when internal human weaknesses allow, or in a few acute emergencies (plague, earthquake, volcano) or in disease – germs replace tigers. *Internal pressures:* need to know and understand, to find a purpose, to explain one's own behaviour; trade and political competition; envy; war.

Responses

Relative freedom from external pressure allowed development of rational knowledge; philosophical questions, ways of argument, enquiry into causation, scientific speculation and observation. Beginnings of critical accounts of own society. Sport linked to war needs. Technical developments in architecture, etc. Applied and theoretical maths. Religion 'humanized' and polytheistic, concept of Fate, Mythology. Drama, music, art.

Departments providing evidence: as before. Good opportunities for acting the themes of Greek tragedy; *Iliad, Odyssey*. Scope for co-operation between technical and art work. Costume for the needlecraft dept., etc, etc.

YEARS FOUR AND FIVE

The Modern Age

Section One

External pressures that still remain: world examples of hunger, disease, poverty, massive waste of errors in agriculture and in uses of technical resources. The urgent problems of over-population; the dangers of war through chance; pollution.

Internal pressures: awareness of ignorance; distrust and paranoia; lack of self-knowledge; isolation in an indifferent universe; fears of other men, of disease, of nuclear war; self-exploitation – drugs, brainwashing, profiteering, power-seeking; fear of death.

Responses: medicine, agriculture, industry, applied science, education, psychology, political attempts at unity, pure science, exploration of space and enquiries about the origins of the universe. Philosophy and religion.

Section Two

Applications:
Our own society –
    (a) a picture of individual personality development
    (b) the family and personal relationships
    (c) the behaviour of groups (prejudice, loyalty, co-operation, etc.)

Our own neighbourhood –
    (a) a sociological survey
    (b) responses to its needs – what human problems need to be solved?
    (c) its art, architecture, music, recreations – are we satisfied?

(d) a comparison with conditions a century earlier. What sort of progress is still needed?

(e) our political structure, local and national, compared with other nations.

Are our responses adequate? Do we make the best use of our wealth, our knowledge and our power? Do we use our leisure fruitfully?

Speculations:

The future of our society. What pressures do we envisage?

What responses can or must be made?

What have we learned from recent history – the industrial revolution, the wars, racial persecution, nazism?

What hopeful responses are to be seen?

Various ideas of utopia.

N.B. The implementation of such a scheme in the fourth and fifth years would demand very close gearing of the different departments, though the basic work would be done in the lessons specifically allocated to thematic studies. Throughout the course numerous small projects can be employed – for example, the translation of personal research into: notes and charts to show social organization; folders of examples of good and bad architecture or design; folders on important 'responses' – e.g. discovery, invention, scientific theories, etc., etc.

I have quoted extensively from Roland Harris's paper hoping that his general ideas for the 'content' of the curriculum will illustrate the practicality of putting such an ambitious scheme into operation. But the 'content' could vary dramatically according to the interests of the staff and the pupils, to the locality of the school, and to the facilities available. What really matters is the way in which 'thematic studies' can be the basis of the whole school curriculum, and help pupils to be educated as *people*.

There could be no better exercise, at this stage, for a future teacher than to envisage how the scheme could be put into operation in any school with which he is familiar.

PART TWO

Education and Values

six

Value Judgements

It is now time to take a closer look at the nature of value judgements, for all important questions about education are ultimately questions about values.

To begin with, we must distinguish between two uses of the word 'good', as in (*a*) 'Is this a good way to teach spelling?' and (*b*) 'Is critical thinking a good thing to foster in pupils?'

In (*a*) 'good' means something like 'efficient'. A 'good' way of teaching spelling is one which efficiently achieves its aim. In this case we are dealing with the kind of issue that can be put to a test: it is a matter of *fact* whether one method of achieving a certain aim is more efficient than another. But in (*b*) the word good is being used in a *moral* sense. One might agree that critical thinking is a 'good' aim in itself, that it is intrinsically a worth-while activity. One could also argue that critical thinking is good in an *instrumental* sense: that if the majority of people are capable of thinking critically this will help them to achieve a successful democratic society. And in this way one has deferred one's value judgement: now it may be necessary to justify *democracy* as a goal. Again one might regard democracy as a good thing in itself but go further and say that democracy is also *instrumentally* good in, say, creating the greatest happiness for the greatest possible number of people. And still one is left with the need for a value judgement: is the greatest happiness for the greatest number of people a *good* aim?

Similarly, in a discussion of comprehensive schools, one may argue that they promote equality of educational opportunity – they are not 'good' *in themselves* but are instrumentally good in achieving a certain aim. And the next value judgement concerns equality of opportunity, which is perhaps *intrinsically* good and/or which may help to achieve a 'good' form of society.

Now whereas one can *prove* certain sorts of statements to be true or false this does not appear to apply to *value judgements*.

There are ways of proving that twice six is twelve, or that water is composed of oxygen and hydrogen: but there is no way of 'proving' that it is morally bad to break a promise, or that one painting is better than another.

To understand why this is so it is necessary to look more closely at different sorts of statements, or propositions. The term *proposition* can for our purposes be taken to mean a statement which one cannot utter *without committing oneself to denying contradictions of that statement.*

Thus if one asserts this proposition 'Mount Everest is the highest mountain in the world' one *must* also *deny* that it is *not* the highest mountain in the world.

(Not all statements are propositions in this strict sense. For example, one could say both 'Love makes the world go round' and 'Love does not make the world go round' without really contradicting oneself. This is because the first statement is not meant literally.)

Some propositions, known as *analytic* propositions, are true or false simply because of the meaning of the words which compose them. For example, the proposition 'No bachelors are married' is true because 'bachelor' *means* 'an unmarried person'. To verify the proposition one does not need to go round questioning bachelors; one only needs to understand the component words. Other examples of analytic propositions are: 'Triangles have three sides' and 'Teetotallers do not knowingly drink alcohol'.

Other propositions, known as *synthetic* propositions, one can show to be true or false only by investigating the physical world. For example, the proposition 'All bachelors have red hair' can be shown to be false as soon as one bachelor is found whose hair is *not* red. Such a proposition is not true or false because of the meaning of the component words but because of their relationship to observable phenomena.

Other examples of synthetic propositions are: 'Mount Everest is the highest mountain in the world', and 'Shakespeare was a poet and playwright'.

Both analytic and synthetic propositions, then, can be shown to be true or false provided that they are meaningful: in the first case one needs to investigate the meaning of the component words, and in the second case one needs to investigate the real world.

Unfortunately it does not seem to be the case that either of these tests can tell us if *value* judgements are true or false, and it is very important to understand why this is so.

In the first place it seems highly unlikely that aesthetic or moral judgements could be labelled *analytic*, for analytic propositions can tell us nothing new about the world* that could not be derived from the nature of the terms used. And if I say, 'As a playwright, Marlowe achieved less than Shakespeare', or 'You ought not to have broken the promise you made yesterday' I am obviously saying things which could *not* be proved simply by defining each word in each sentence. I could give reasons to support my judgements, but these reasons would involve reference to a whole range of concepts which were not contained in the wording of the original judgements. Some statements about morality may *appear* to be analytic, but inevitably they will turn out to be trivial. For example, the statement 'Murder is always wrong' can be shown to be true if you define 'murder' as 'wrong killing', for the statement then means simply 'wrong killing is wrong'. To make a genuine moral judgement one would have to say what kind of killings are *wrong* killings, and to do this one would have to introduce new concepts that are *not* already present in the sentence 'Murder is always wrong'.

In the second place there are difficulties about thinking of judgements as being *synthetic* propositions. For if synthetic propositions (like 'Mount Everest is the highest mountain in the world')

* This statement would be disputed by certain philosophers, but there is no space here to go into the highly complex arguments on both sides.

can be verified by discovering certain *facts*, then it should also be possible to show that aesthetic and moral *judgements* can be verified in the same way, i.e. if you say that one painting is 'better' than another all you have to do is produce certain facts and your case is proved once and for all.

Now philosophers have tried for thousands of years to show that moral judgements can be verified by reference to facts, and none has ever succeeded. Theories of this sort may loosely be called 'naturalistic' theories because they are based on the idea that there are facts in nature which *make* moral judgements true or false. Here are some examples of such theories:

1. *Hedonism*

It is a 'fact' that if we do certain things we feel happier as a consequence, and the things that in the long run contribute to our happiness are the 'right' things to do.

There are many snags about this doctrine, though it can be made to sound very convincing. The main snags are:

(*a*) Common sense tells us that we often feel actions to be 'right' or 'wrong' without apparently taking into account any question of happiness or pleasure. For example, if I condemn fox hunting I do so because of its effects on foxes, not primarily because *I* feel happier in consequence.

(*b*) If happiness is a consequence of doing the 'right' thing, one still needs other criteria for judging whether the action is 'right' in the first place. For example, I might well feel happy (afterwards) that I had plunged into a fire to save a child's life, but only because I already knew it was the right thing to do.

(*c*) People do not always know what will make them happy; but even if they did, and acted *only* on this principle, we would be tempted to say that they weren't acting *morally* at all: they would simply be pursuing happiness and perhaps doing the 'right' thing purely by chance.

2. *Utilitarianism*

'Good' actions are those which lead to the greatest possible happiness for the greatest possible number of people.

The same objections apply. Even if one could work out what would bring the greatest happiness one still needs other reasons for deciding that this is the *right* thing to do. And inevitably there is the hidden assumption that what is *morally* right is what will bring the 'best sort' of happiness – so one must have one's own criteria for deciding what is 'morally right' and what is the 'best sort' of happiness.

3. *Divine Will*

God made the world in a certain sort of way; God is good, so the 'natural' order of things is good. Specifically, if one knows what God approves of, then this must be the right thing to do.

There are many objections to this point of view, some of which concern (*a*) the problem of how to decide what is 'natural', (*b*) the moral position of atheists, and (*c*) the problem of how to know what God approves of.

But basically the problem is that, in order to say 'Good actions are those of which God approves', one is *already* committed to a moral judgement, namely that God *is* good. In order to believe this one must already be using moral criteria which are independent of believing in some form of deity, for one could logically believe in a god who sometimes did wicked things. And since the only reasonable basis for believing that God is good is to judge that what He does (and approves of) is good one would merely be going round in circles to say that one knows what is good *because* it is approved by God.

All naturalistic theories of morality have one thing in common – they attempt to translate *moral* words like 'good' into *factual terms*. Instead of saying that a man is *good* one could give a list of facts (such as: he obeys the law, he is truthful, he tries to make people happy, etc.). But this leads to another important objection to naturalism. If saying that a man is good is the *same* as saying he does x, y and z then we have deprived ourselves of one very important function of the word 'good', the function of *commending*. By saying that a man is good we are normally *com-*

mending him for doing x, y and z, i.e. we are saying 'It is good that
he does x, y and z'. But if 'good' *means* doing 'x, y and z' we
cannot do this: we can only say 'He does x, y and z'.

Another sort of theory about morality comes under the general
heading of 'non-naturalistic'. According to this one does not judge
the goodness of an action by noting additional facts about it (such
as the fact that it leads to more happiness) but rather one has a
direct intuition of its goodness. Just as one can *see* that an object is
yellow, so one can see intuitively that an action is good.

Various philosophers have given attractive arguments in favour
of this view, and it is not possible to consider these arguments here.
The obvious snag is that different people have different intuitions,
and if this is the *only* way of making a moral judgement then there
can be no way of settling any moral argument. For if one person
'knows' by intuition that capital punishment is justifiable, and
another 'knows' that it isn't, then they have no extra way of judging which intuition is right.

A great deal of controversy was caused in the first half of this
century by philosophers who popularized an extreme view about
moral judgements which became satirically known as the 'boo-
hurrah' theory. Roughly, they said that words like 'good' and
'bad' did no more than express the *feelings* of the speaker. If one
says, 'Lying is bad' all one is doing really is to say, 'Lying – boo!',
and if one says, 'Truthfulness is good' one is really only saying,
'Truthfulness, hurrah!'.

Again, an attempt is being made to get rid of moral terms by
translating them into factual terms. 'x is good' becomes the same
as 'I approve of x', and 'x is bad' becomes the same as 'I disapprove of x'. And again, if the theory were correct, there would be
no point in moral discourse, because there would be no way of
settling any moral argument. People could merely accept that
they felt one way or the other.

Now commonsense tells us that when people make a statement
like 'It is bad to kill people for personal gain' they are *not* just
talking about their own feelings. If I say 'I don't like parsnips' I

am making a purely individual statement about my own feelings,
but if I say 'It is bad to kill people for gain' I must also say 'One
ought not to kill people for gain'. And if I say this I am doing at
least two things:

(*a*) I am prescribing a course of action for myself (I will not kill
people for gain), and
(*b*) I am prescribing a course of action for *other* people (Do not
kill for gain).

We can now see why moral judgements cannot be verified in
the same way as statements, for whereas *statements* (like 'Water
contains oxygen') con logically be described as true or false, *commands* (like 'close the door') cannot logically be so described. And
it does seem that one function of a moral judgement is more akin
to a command than to a statement.

However, if moral judgements were *merely* a form of command
it would still not be possible to hold fruitful arguments about
morality – nothing would be achieved by two people giving each
other conflicting commands, except that the more powerful could
perhaps impose his will.

What we are looking for still are criteria for judging moral
judgements – we want to be able to say that we are *right* in
judging that one ought not to kill people for gain.

In an attempt to solve this problem some modern philosophers
(notably R. M. Hare in *The Language of Morals* and *Freedom
and Reason*, O.U.P.) have developed the idea that as well as being
prescriptive genuine moral judgements must also be *univer-
salizable*. This means that if one makes a particular moral judgement (He ought not to do x) then one must also make the same
judgement about *anyone* (including oneself) in the same situation.

Here is a simple example. You are driving towards the brow of
a hill and narrowly avoid an oncoming car which had been
overtaking a lorry. You might simply think 'Damned fool!' which
is merely an expression of your own feelings. But you might also
make a *judgement* to the effect that he *ought* not to have been

overtaking in that particular place. Now if this is a genuine moral judgement it can be universalized – no driver ought to overtake when he can't see the road ahead. You are *prescribing* that neither you nor anyone else should do this. And it is the fact that you can assent to this universalization that makes the original judgement a genuinely moral one. If you simply felt that *he* shouldn't do it but that *you* are entitled to do it, then your original remark loses its moral status. In a sense you were misusing the word 'ought'. You merely meant 'I don't like him doing that'.

Here is another example. A trumpeter happens to like practising at all hours of the night, and consequently disturbs his neighbours, who dislike the trumpet and want to get some sleep. Now if he invoked the principle of 'Do by others as you would be done by' he might reply, 'Well, that's O.K. – *they*'re welcome to play the trumpet all night, I wouldn't mind'. But this reply does not meet the demands of universalization, for if he assents to *this* judgement: 'I am entitled to keep non-trumpet-lovers awake against their wishes' he must *also* assent to the judgement: 'If I were a non-trumpet-lover who wanted to sleep at night, the trumpeter next door would be entitled to do just what *I* was doing'. And if he rejects this he must also reject the first judgement, for genuinely moral judgements must be impartial.

One more example, an extreme one. A particular German says: 'It is right to kill any person of Jewish descent'. Now if he really means this to be a moral judgement (and not just an expression of hatred) he must also assent to the judgement that if *he* were of Jewish descent then he too should be killed. And as Professor Hare said, if one tricked him into believing that in fact he *was* of Jewish descent it is most unlikely that he would accept the latter judgement. He may still go on killing Jews, but at least he can no longer claim that this is morally justifiable.

The attraction of this approach to morality is that instead of being concerned with general moral rules (like 'Be truthful') it provides a criterion for each case in which a moral judgement has to be made.

It is dangerous for people to rely on general moral rules because there are inevitably situations where they should not be applied (as, for example, when someone would be justified in telling a lie). This is why any authoritarian system of ethics may lead to intolerance and injustice – people may become more concerned with obeying rules for their own sake than in doing what is morally right.

The obvious snag about the concept of universalizability is that it is very difficult to apply except in uncomplicated situations. Certainly it seems a sound logical criterion for testing whether a judgement *is* moral, but in purely practical terms it need not be particularly helpful.

Suppose, for example, that a married man is considering the morality of having an affair with his secretary. One thought that may cross his mind is that he wouldn't like his wife to have an affair with *her* boss, but this is not strictly to the point. What he *should* ask himself is: 'If I were in my wife's situation, and were exactly the same sort of person that she is, how would I feel about my husband having an affair with his secretary?'

But even if he decided that she would be made very unhappy, he may still be uncertain what moral judgement to make. He may decide that the pleasure of the affair is more important than the pain to the wife (in which case he would have to agree that even if he were the suffering wife he ought to approve of the affair). Or he may decide that the *deceit* involved would be the significant moral issue (in which case he could argue that 'It is not justifiable to deceive my wife since if I were her I could not approve of my husband deceiving me'). But it would then be a separate issue whether he should simply tell his wife the whole truth and carry on with the affair.

Whatever judgement he makes can be tested for universalizability, but it is obvious that even commonplace situations would defy moral analysis of this sort by an unintelligent person.

seven

Mores and Morality

SOME readers may have found the last chapter difficult, especially if they had no previous knowledge of philosophy. Since I shall next try to show the relevance of value judgements to the work of the teacher, it would perhaps be a good idea to bridge the gap between theory and practice by summarizing some points about morality in a more popular sense of that term.

The *mores* of a particular society are a set of customs or conventions which are imbued with an ethical significance. Within any set of mores there will be a sort of scale of importance. At the top end of the scale there will probably be powerful sanctions against murder, theft and incest, and in favour of honesty, truthfulness and respect for parents. At the bottom end of the scale come issues which we would perhaps regard as matters of etiquette, concerning, for example, guests belching after meals, or men opening doors for women.

Generally speaking there is a great deal in common between the 'high priority' mores of different societies, but the further you go down the scale the more variety you find. Incest is universally abhorred, but belching after a meal may be either polite or rude according to the locality.

Somewhere between the two extremes come issues which it may be difficult to define either as 'morally important' or as 'merely etiquette'. In this country, at the present time, nudity is such an issue. Is it *immoral* to sunbathe naked in the local park? Or would it just be a breach of etiquette? At the beginning of the century it would have been thought immoral. By the end of the century it may not be a moral issue at all.

This middle part of the scale presents particular problems to people who visit other cultures. On some issues it seems that one should be prepared to do in Rome as the Romans do – few people would feel that it was 'immoral' to laugh and dance during a funeral procession, if that were the local custom. On the other hand one would probably draw the line at joining a head-hunting expedition.

Between the two extremes, however, one might not be at all sure whether an issue was 'moral' or not. Travellers have, for example, been baffled by the problem of what to do if the host, an Eskimo, courteously offers his wife for the night. A more familiar problem faces many young people when they start work at a factory where there are long-standing traditions of minor fiddling – misusing the firm's time, or taking 'perks' in the form of small items useful at home. If the firm turns a blind eye to this sort of activity has it become part of an unofficial 'arrangement' between employer and employee? Or is it always to be deplored?

In a so-called 'permissive' society people of orthodox views become conscious that certain sanctions are losing their force, are sliding down the scale of importance, so that matters which were once considered of grave moral importance become widely regarded as mere conventions. In Britain today right-wingers are concerned about such issues as promiscuity, divorce, drug-taking, lack of parental control, and so on. Once it was an unspeakable offence for a girl to have premarital intercourse: nowadays, in some circumstances, few people would condemn her severely.

But people who bewail the permissive society tend to forget that there is also a movement *up* the scale of a whole variety of sanctions. Not long ago it would have been a rare act of courtesy if the builders of a new estate had shown their plans to other houseowners in the area: now, their plans are subject to all sorts of laws and regulations designed to protect the general public. We are more *restrictive* in many ways. We insist that all children attend school until they are 16, we try to prevent racial discrimination by law, we fight against the economic exploitation of women and children, we try to stop people spoiling the landscape, we forbid

F

the hunting of certain animals and birds, we punish people for drunken driving more severely than ever before, we have made laws against undesirable mergers and against misleading advertising.

Generally speaking we are (*a*) abandoning those mores which interfere unnecessarily with the freedom of the individual, but (*b*) are creating new ones which are meant to *protect* the individual from being harmed or restricted by others. These changes are reflected in recent legislation concerning (*a*) homosexuality, divorce and abortion, and (*b*) misleading descriptions of goods or services for sale, and standards of hygiene in food production.

It should be apparent by now that the words 'mores' and 'morality' are quite different in meaning. The distinction can be brought out sharply when one talks of being *morally* critical of certain *mores*. For example, we no longer approve of slavery, of an inferior status for women, or of child labour, even though they were all acceptable as part of the mores of our society until quite recently. Not even the 'high priority' *mores* can be taken as sure moral truths, as can be seen from the fact that the subjection of women has been almost universally approved in the past.

To conform to popular opinion is not, therefore, necessarily to act morally. It is usually *expedient* to conform, and one may have other practical reasons for so doing (or even lack the imagination *not* to conform). But to act *morally* in any given situation involves (*a*) taking into account the needs of other people, (*b*) deliberately and freely choosing one course of action rather than another, and (*c*) acting only on a principle which one would approve for anyone else in the same situation.

eight

Moral Education

DISPUTES about the role of R.E. in schools tend to throw up the extreme views that it should either remain a compulsory part of the curriculum or be completely replaced by something called 'moral education' or 'education in personal relationships'. Such disputes are often futile because those involved have no very clear idea of what they *mean* by the terms they are using. In particular, some people seem to think that 'moral education' means 'religious education minus religion'. And often the terms 'moral instruction' or 'moral training' are used indiscriminately.

Now if we took these terms at their face value, *moral instruction* would mean something like 'getting people to learn the facts about the mores of their society (and perhaps of other societies), including the "facts" about what is right and what is wrong'. The first part of this definition is certainly a *part* of moral education, as we shall see; but the second part does not make sense because morality is not a collection of *facts* that can be learned by heart. *Moral training* would mean something like 'bringing up children so that they conform to "good" principles of behaviour'. But we have seen that genuine moral choices must be both free and rational. It is of course possible to condition people to feel guilty about doing certain things and to feel obliged to do other things, but this is not *education*. In the first place there is the assumption that the teacher knows beyond doubt that he is right about morality. In the second place a person who responded to this sort of training would not be acting *morally* at all (just as a cat is not acting 'morally' if it ceases to jump on to the dining table after its owner has smacked it on each attempt). Of course one has to train small children to behave in a way which is socially acceptable until they are old enough to think for themselves, but it would be more precise to call this a process of *socialization* rather than one of moral training.

It seemed profitable, in the first chapter, to consider the nature of education in the light of what qualities we would expect to find in an educated person. The parallel step now is to ask what qualities one would look for in a *morally* educated person. If we can reach some agreement about this, the next step is to ask what sort of education would foster such qualities.

John Wilson, in *An Introduction to Moral Education,* suggests that being morally educated is a complex concept involving six components. Since the language we normally use in talk about morality tends to be vague and ambiguous he has invented six new terms for these attributes, each of which comes from a Greek root. They are rather ugly-sounding terms, but at least they have a precise meaning.

(a) PHIL: the attitude that the feelings and needs of other people are equally important with one's own

(b) EMP: the ability to have insight into other people's feelings (ALLEMP) and into one's own feelings (AUTEMP)

(c) GIG: 1. the possession of enough factual information to be able to predict the consequences of one's actions
          2. the ability to communicate one's thoughts and feelings to other people

(d) DIK: the ability to form principles of behaviour in relation to other people's needs

(e) PHRON: the ability to form principles of behaviour in relation to one's own needs

(f) KRAT: 1. sensitivity to situations needing a moral decision
          2. the resolution to act in accordance with one's principles

PHIL is clearly fundamental to moral behaviour, for if one did not regard other people as being as important as oneself one would not need to act *morally* at all. There would be no compulsion to universalize judgements or to put oneself in the other person's shoes. PHIL can vary in two ways – strength and range. A person who very strongly believes in equality will be more influenced by it in his actual behaviour than one who merely pays lip service to it. And whereas some people accept that *all* other humans are of equal importance most people tend to restrict this attitude to others of the same race, or colour, or social background. In an extreme case a person might accept that members of his own tribe were equally important, but feel entitled to eat people from the tribe next door. Another extreme is the Christian ideal of universal brotherhood.

EMP. We saw in Chapter Five that to be able to universalize a moral judgement it is necessary to be able to see a given situation from someone else's point of view. In the case of the man having doubts about an affair with his secretary he needed to put himself in his wife's shoes and imagine what her feeling would be. Insight of this sort is clearly a necessary part of forming particular moral judgements. If one had no idea of what sort of things pleased other people, or what made them jealous, angry or hurt, how could one possibly put oneself in their shoes? And one who did not have reasonable insight into his *own* feelings would be like a small child, unable to evaluate his desires in the light of reason.

Of course EMP *alone* would not necessarily promote moral behaviour. One could have great insight into people, but use this simply to gain selfish power over them. But if one also has the attitude PHIL one could not regard this as the right thing to do.

GIG (1) is vital in the sense that if one never *could* predict the outcome of one's actions one would be deprived of the raw material of moral judgements. One might love one's cat, yet kill it with kindness through simple ignorance of its needs. A teacher might be well-disposed towards his pupils, but do them more harm than good through misunderstanding their level of emotional and conceptual development. A person ignorant of the laws and customs of his society could get himself and others into all sorts of dire trouble, however well he meant. Moral thinking *necessitates* working out the consequences of one's actions.

GIG (2) is important because morality is an interpersonal affair. If one has difficulty in communicating one's emotions, desires and thoughts one's effectiveness as a moral agent is bound to be diminished – if only because other people will have insufficient (or misleading) data about *your* needs.

DIK and PHRON, the ability to form principles of behaviour, may be compared to the skill of a well trained batsman. Under real conditions of play the batsman has to rely on a sort of built-in set of batting principles – for he certainly has no time to *work out* what to do when facing a fast bowler. But it is not *instinct* he relies on; there is no such thing as a *born* batsman. Rather he has learned over a long period of time what works and what doesn't work, and provided nothing entirely new happens he can rely on his batting 'reflex'. If, on the other hand, he goes to Australia and plays for the first time on a very hard wicket in a very dry atmosphere he may find that his reflex fails him – he has to start learning again.

In the same way we develop a sort of moral reflex, for in real life we could not possibly stop and think about each situation we encounter. But if it is a *sound* moral reflex it is not simply an emotional reaction, or the promptings of conscience. Rather we have learned that certain responses are appropriate in certain sorts of situation. So when familiar situations recur we don't need to rethink all the issues involved. If one was incapable of recognizing that a new situation closely resembled a previous one* then one would be as badly off as the batsman who was surprised each time that a leg-break followed a particular movement of the bowler's wrist.

KRAT (1) is the ability to recognize that certain situations *are* new and require new factors to be taken into account. To pursue the cricket analogy, an imaginative batsman playing for the first time in Austrialia would at least be particularly cautious, and could seek advice from more experienced players as well as getting some practice in the nets before playing in an important match.

* Existentialists have this trouble, possibly because few of them seem to play cricket.

The reader can doubtless work out what this means in moral terms.

Lastly, KRAT (2), the resolution to act on one's principles. All that need be said at this point is that it would be very odd to describe a person as being morally educated if he were so weak-willed that he very seldom *did* what he thought was right.

Various objections have been put forward to this analysis, but this is not a book on moral philosophy and there is not space to go into them properly. But one very common criticism is worth mentioning because it is so often the first reaction of people who have not previously given much thought to the subject. 'This is all very well,' they say, 'but you seem to be claiming that you have to be *clever* to be good. Surely this isn't so. There are plenty of good *simple* people around.'

The answers to this objection are:

1. John Wilson is analysing what it means to be *morally educated*, not what is meant to be 'good' – a much vaguer term. A simple person may well lead a 'good' simple life provided that he is not called upon to make judgements of matters outside his familiar environment, and provided his environment is secure and relatively unchanging. But moral *education* implies the flexibility to cope with quite new situations (as everyone has to who lives in such a rapidly evolving society as our own).

2. A second look at the six components should convince you that cleverness (in the sense of possessing a high I.Q.) is not really in demand. Certainly it requires intelligence to be able to predict the consequences of one's actions, but otherwise it would be more to the point to say that people of *abnormally* low intelligence are bound to be handicapped in their moral development than to say that it requires a high degree of intelligence to be 'good'.

It is now apparent that moral education cannot possibly be any one particular sort of process. The components are so various that a whole battery of different processes are involved.

As far as the individual teacher is concerned perhaps EMP is the component which he can most readily help to develop in his pupils. Any good teacher of literature is incidentally fostering greater insight into how people think, feel and react. From literature not only does one gain understanding of a much greater range of people and situations than one will ever encounter in life, but also one can gain a deeper understanding of *familiar* situations. From *The Diary of Anne Frank,* for example, one learns not only about the reactions of a Jewish family hiding from persecution under extreme circumstances, but also about the emotional development of *any* adolescent girl.

Participation in drama is another powerful form of education. When children in a primary school improvise a play about family life – based, for example, on the visit of a nagging grandmother – they are not just acting: they are finding out to some extent what it feels like to *live* the different roles involved.

It is also increasingly common for children to be brought into contact with a wide range of people outside the school. Pupils who help to decorate the house of a bedridden old-age-pensioner may incidentally learn something about the problems of age, isolation and poverty. Adolescents helping in a local nursery school will learn something about the emotional needs of small children.

The strength of PHIL (the attitude that the feelings and needs of others are equally important as one's own) is doubtless largely determined by early home background. But a child's tendency to adopt the attitude must be considerably strengthened, if only at an unconscious level, if he perceives that it is an attitude which is not only shared by adults but which also influences their treatment of others.

Probably the *range* of PHIL can be extended by much the same methods that apply to EMP. If one feels that one has no obligations of any kind towards certain groups of people (the Chinese, the blacks, the mentally ill, criminals, communists, etc.) it is usually because of prejudice, ignorance, or both. A person who is reasonably well-informed about the causes of mental illness, and who is well acquainted with a variety of mentally ill people, is not likely to make remarks like: 'They should all be kept locked up' or 'They should all be sterilized'. And anyone who is widely acquainted with Russia, and has Russian friends, is not likely to regard Russians *en masse* as a menace that should be wiped out if only there were no fear of retaliation.

In schools, therefore, it seems reasonable to suppose that the range of PHIL may be extended by the intelligent use of books, films and television programmes which bring greater imaginative understanding of different cultures, classes and creeds.

GIG (1) demands, among other things, adequate knowledge of one's society's laws, customs and etiquette. These, of course, lie in the provinces of current affairs, social studies, R.E., 'general studies', and so on. But children can be well-informed yet *still* not think of their actions in terms of the consequences to other people. The Schools Council Moral Education Project in Oxford has been considering this problem (among others) and is about to publish some interesting suggestions concerning ways in which teachers can encourage pupils to use their imagination in predicting the possible outcome of various forms of anti-social behaviour.

GIG (2), the ability to communicate one's thoughts and emotions, is increasingly fostered in schools thanks to recent emphasis on oracy. Traditional grammar schools have usually done very little to help pupils to express themselves (except on paper), but current trends in drama teaching (especially with regard to 'free' drama where the pupils have maximum opportunity to express themselves through improvisation) are helping to redress the balance. Also, new concepts of physical education are emphasizing self-expression rather than perpetuating the old routines of physical exercise.

The ability to form principles of behaviour (DIK and PHRON) is perhaps particularly accessible to more direct forms of moral education (via discussion in English or R.E. lessons).

Most teenagers, asked to give reasons for their moral attitudes, quote 'principles' that they have *acquired*. They are not used to the idea that there can be a rational basis for moral behaviour, and tend to give a whole variety of reasons which are not really *moral* reasons at all. Some of them tend to give self-centred expedient reasons. They might say that stealing was wrong because 'I might be caught and punished', or 'I'd feel ashamed'. Others give reasons which refer the judgement to some form of authority. 'It's against the law' or 'My parents have taught me stealing is wrong'. Others are 'moral conformists': 'None of my friends or family would steal'. Surprisingly few can go straight to the heart of the matter and give reasons which take into account the feelings and needs of the *victims* of the theft, or the effects of wide-spread stealing on society in general.

One part of the teacher's task, then, is to show pupils that some of their ideas are superficial or ill-founded – a process which can be painful, especially in the case of teenagers who think that conscience provides the last word on moral issues. But the positive part of the task is to help pupils to form their *own* principles which logically must be based on PHIL, EMP, GIG and KRAT (1); and the first step towards this is to convince them that (*a*) having principles involves having genuine reasons for one's moral attitudes, and (*b*) that if one makes a moral judgement one is not just *talking*, but committing oneself to a course of *action*.

Lastly, KRAT. Helping people to be resolute in doing what they think is right is perhaps the hardest task in moral education. More will be said about this in the next chapter, but the key factor would seem to be the amount of responsibility given to children in the school context. It is not sufficient that a few pupils should be selected as prefects – every pupil can be given responsibility of some sort in influencing the running of the school and in the organization of his own work. This applies even in primary schools. And it is the opportunity to exercise power, and to live with the consequences of one's decisions, that is likely to develop KRAT (2).

(Incidentally, I have not talked specifically about the role of the teacher in fostering AUTEMP, insight into one's own feelings. Perhaps readers would like to consider the particular relevance of (*a*) creative writing, (*b*) drama, and (*c*) art.)

I hope it is now apparent that moral education is not a 'subject' which could be covered by three or four periods a week on the timetable. Certainly it is not merely a possible substitute for R.E. Moral education in the richest sense can only be achieved by imaginative integration of the whole school curriculum. And every teacher of every subject should be aware of the different sorts of contribution he can make.

Our society has reached a crucial phase of development where young people are justifiably reacting against traditional, authoritarian values without always being able to survive in the resulting moral vacuum. No task of the teacher can be more important than helping them to generate for themselves a healthier atmosphere in which to create a new society.

Interlude 3

EVERY pupil at Blackmore Secondary Modern was aware that Miss Gifkins' rat was about to give birth; and Mr James (the head of the science department) was becoming increasingly exasperated about the way he was missing part of his precious tea-break each day through having to drive curious children out of the laboratory. He was unused to children being curious, and found it extremely tiresome.

This situation had arisen because he had decided to give Miss Gifkins the privilege of taking 4C for Biology; but on the whole he regretted this policy. Although he had gained two free periods a week he now had to share his laboratory with a girl who insisted on bringing nasty smelly creatures into it. For his own part, he had always relied on film slides, which required no feeding and which made no mess for the caretaker to grumble about.

Miss Gifkins' motive in acquiring a pregnant rat was to teach 4C about birth and to use this as a starting point for a spell of sex education. She had once bravely taken the class for a nature walk; and, while she was not altogether surprised to find that half of them had melted away to reassemble in a local transport café, she was disconcerted by the way one boy reappeared from behind a tree wearing on his head a pair of scarlet knickers that she was fairly sure belonged to a very fat, lethargic girl called Deborah Bird. Although her College had given her no guidance on sex education, Miss Gifkins felt that the time had come to use some initiative. Some knowledge of birth, intercourse and contraception, she thought, could be followed by some frank discussion of sexual morality.

The rat was a great success, especially with the first-formers; and Miss Gifkins began to find that many of them joined her during her daily walk to school to ask the same questions over and over again: 'When will the babies come?' 'How many will there be?' 'How do they come out? Can we watch?'

She was therefore somewhat disconcerted when the Headmaster, making his annual foray into the school at large, expressed an interest in the rat but added: 'Of course, if the Event occurs during school time, you'll have to turn the cage to the wall. It wouldn't do for the children to *see*, you know. Could be awfully – you know – *awkward*. They might very well start asking questions.'

Fortunately (for the sake of peace and quiet) the birth took place during the night, and the next time 4C arrived for Biology, there were fifteen baby rats for them to admire.

In fact, things went fairly quietly while she drew diagrams of a developing foetus, first in a rat, and then in a human; and when she invited questions there was total silence.

Eventually, Billy Davis spoke. 'Miss,' he asked, 'why don't we ever have no sex education?'

'Well this *is* sex education,' replied Miss Gifkins.

'Nah I don't mean about babies,' he said scornfully.

'What *do* you mean?'

'You know, *sex* education.'

A girl sitting next to him slapped his hand impatiently. 'Leave her alone,' she said. 'She isn't *married*, is she? What does *she* know?' 'Nor was your sister married,' he replied, 'but *she* must have known enough.'

Miss Gifkins pretended not to have heard, and, recalling advice given in a television programme, invited the class to write down any questions they would like to be answered. Several of the girls refused to write anything at all (one of them said she didn't mind *listening,* but she didn't want to *think* about it); but in the end she was handed about eighteen slips of paper from which she eliminated eight immediately as being either illegible or obscene. The ten remaining questions were:

(1) How long does it take to have it up

(2) What courses a miss carrige
(3) Waht is a johnny?
(4) Why do girls skwork if you touch her up?
(5) How many pills do you need first.
(6) Is it trew that if your PREGNANT and jump off of a chair it brings it off?
(7) Please, how deos intercorse tak plas
(8) What exactly do you do with a durrecks?
(9) Why do girls have perriods
(10) Does it mater how big it is??

Miss Gifkins was suddenly aware that there were quite a few gaps in her knowledge of the English language, but she was determined not to be thrown off balance.

'Judging from these questions,' she said firmly, 'some of you just wanted to embarrass me, and some of you want to ask sensible questions but don't know the right words to use.' She suddenly felt priggish at the last remark, but really she could never bring herself to use the expression 'have it up'. Ugh! 'I think we'd better start at the beginning with some diagrams of the sex organs.'

She drew some appropriate cross-sections on the blackboard, and explained at length the function of the ovaries and testicles. 'And then, so that the sperm can get to the ovum, the male places his penis in the vagina, here, and the released sperm swim upwards till one of them gets inside the ovum and fertilizes it. Any questions so far? It's almost time for the bell.'

In the class, there were about half a dozen boys who were virtually totally ignorant about sex, but only one of them, Frank Bell, was unsophisticated enough to admit it.

'Please, miss,' he asked, 'how do *people* do it?'

Monica Perkins was stirred to speak.

'Don't be daft,' she said; 'she's *talking* about bleeding people. Haven't you ever looked at yourself?'

'I don't look like *that*.'

'That's what you'd look like if you got a kitchen knife and slit yourself up the middle,' Monica explained with infinite patience.

Miss Gifkins was inspired. 'Perhaps *you*'d like to come and explain the diagrams, Monica,' she suggested.

'No I would *not,* miss. I think it's *dirty*, talking about it in cold blood. Why don't he just find out for himself like anyone else?'

Several of the girls expressed agreement with Monica's empirical approach, and Miss Gifkins made a mental note to get on to contraception as soon as possible.

Frank Bell was still not satisfied. 'I still don't see how it goes in, the way you've drawn it.'

'Oh, gawd, can I show him, miss?'

Privately, Miss Gifkins thought that this was an excellent idea; but as the bell went at that moment Monica was temporarily delayed from embarking on her future career.

nine

Sex Education

IT may seem rather odd, in so short a book, to devote a whole chapter to sex education while ignoring very controversial issues concerning, for example, i.t.a., modern maths., the secondary school examination system, and so on. I do so because the main aim of the book is to clarify the concept of education rather than to discuss methodology; and sex education is a particularly interesting area in that there is considerable confusion about its scope and aims.

Of course, sex education is not a *subject* any more than, for example, 'domestic science' is. Domestic science is an arbitrary gathering together, under one department, of diverse knowledge and skills relevant to running a home. Obvious essentials, for most people, are child-care, needlework, first-aid, household budgeting, and some basic 'do-it-yourself' knowledge of domestic electricity, plumbing and interior decoration. I say that it is an *arbitrary* selection because, really, *everything* one learns is relevant to running a home, and there is no reason why one should exclude art, mathematics, physics, chemistry, biology, woodwork and metal-work – since all these clearly have their relevant aspects. Nor is there any reason to exclude 'education in personal relationships', since running a home for more than one person depends on good relationships more than anything else.

The fact that 'domestic science' exists as such on the timetable reflects a certain social attitude towards the aims of educating girls. It is assumed that the majority of them will leave school as early as possible, get a routine job to pass away the time till marriage, and then spend the bulk of their time as housewives and mothers; therefore, before they leave school, it is a priority to equip them to cope with their domestic role. It is, of course, extremely important that girls (and boys) should be so prepared; but it is probably true that where parents and teachers have limited expectations of schoolgirls, these expectations are self-fulfilling: the curriculum helps to reinforce the likelihood of early school-leaving, early marriage, and lack of further education. The girls see the immediate relevance of domestic science to their lives but not, perhaps, the relevance of poetry: therefore they co-operate cheerfully in lessons with the right label but go to sleep in English. Readers who have persisted this far can perhaps suggest the beginnings of a solution to this problem.

Sex education, too, is an arbitrary gathering together of topics usually including some aspects of human biology, child-care, and moral advice. If one has sex education as such on the time-table it is bound to be arbitrary, since the kind of sexual relationships we have depends on what kind of *people* we are – therefore *every* educational experience is a part of 'sex education'.

The aims of sex education, when it occurs as a 'subject', are often extremely obscure. A casual observer in some schools could not be blamed for supposing that the main aim was to keep children ignorant and to make them feel guilty about any overtly sexual emotions. More typically, however, the aims seem to be (*a*) to inform children about pregnancy and childbirth (but not human intercourse, contraception, V.D. or sexual deviations), and (*b*) to indoctrinate children with the belief that extra-marital sexual intercourse is always wrong (or at least to inhibit them in pre-marital relationships). I have not yet encountered a school where the primary aim was entirely positive – to help children ultimately to understand, value and enjoy the full range of their sexual experiences as far as this is compatible with the well-being of other people – though to my mind this would be a more desirable aim than the previous ones.

However, there are various civilizing influences at work, and it was very cheering to read the following definition in *Sex*

G

Education in Schools, published by the Church Information Office in 1964:

> Sex education is not a 'subject'; it cannot be 'taught', it should not appear on a school timetable nor be confined to a single embarrassed talk by mother or father. . . . Sex education is the totality of influences which help boys and girls to understand the part sex plays in life and to recognize its physical, spiritual and moral dimensions. It should include reliable knowledge of human reproduction and of the physical and emotional developments in each sex; it should prepare both boys and girls for marriage, family and homemaking; it should help young people with their own present problems; it should look outwards to the wider community which has responsibilities for, and makes demands on, individuals.

However one cares to define 'sexual' relationships it is obvious that one cannot sharply distinguish them from any other sort of inter-personal relationships. It therefore seems more profitable to regard 'sex education' in the wider context of 'education in personal relationships' (which I shall now refer to as EPR to avoid repeating that cumbersome phrase) and to see if there are any specific provisions that should be made in schools.

EPR is itself a rather obscure concept, since again *all* educational experiences are relevant; so for the purposes of this chapter I am going to equate it with the educational processes described in the last chapter as being relevant to *moral* education. This may seem an odd thing to do, since EPR and moral education *sound* as though they refer to very different things; but for my part I cannot think of any *practical* differences. Morality is only one dimension of personal relationships, yet to educate a person morally (as we saw in the last chapter) necessarily involves influencing every aspect of his behaviour towards other people. We come back, then, to the components listed by John Wilson; and I shall now try to show how they will help us to define the aims of 'sex education'.

The first component is that the feelings and needs of other people should count equally with one's own. Just as this is fundamental to *any* sort of moral behaviour, so it is fundamental to so-called 'sexual' morality: the needs and feelings of one's sexual partner are just as important as one's own. All is *not* fair in love and war: one should not *use* other people to gratify one's own desires if this involves any possible harm to them. Girls are not *objects* to be competed for, pursued and conquered. They are not status symbols, the possession of which is justified by the consequent boost to the male ego. Nor are men just machines for providing money or security, or for impregnating would-be mothers.

Given that everyone's needs are equally important (PHIL), the nature of the principles (DIK and PHRON) relevant to sexual behaviour are therefore rational (though of course most people are over-influenced by superstition and primitive taboos): in any sexual relationship one should recognize that the feelings and needs of one's partner, however different these may be from one's own, should nevertheless weigh equally. It would, to take a simple example, be wrong for a man to satisfy his desire for intercourse by convincing a girl that he loved her, if this was not the case: the pleasure to the man could not be counted as important as the possible suffering of the (afterwards) disillusioned girl. A man who believed that he was justified in doing this could not *universalize* this judgement: it is most unlikely that, if he looked at the situation from the girl's point of view, he could approve of the deceit involved. A more complex example is a situation in which a young girl wants to have an affair with an older man irrespective of his feelings towards her: in this case he *should* ask himself if there are possibly any undesirable consequences to the girl – consequences which she is too inexperienced to predict. These and other situations also involve PHRON, a consideration of what is 'right' in relation to one's *own* needs and feelings: one should presumably avoid sexual behaviour which is degrading or damaging to one's own personality, though there are no *rules* which could help any particular individual to know what would be damaging or degrading. One can only say that unfortunate results are likely if in his sexual life a person behaves in ways which are inconsistent with his *general* moral outlook; and unfortunately, in our society, this is very frequently the case.

Some readers may be wishing that I would try to be more specific about the 'rights' and 'wrongs' of sexual behaviour; but it would be inappropriate in this context: if people are morally educated they should be able to work out their own sexual morality for themselves – given adequate factual information. No rules, whatever their source, can be a substitute for moral thinking. Some young people find masturbation degrading: if they were adequately informed about masturbation they might well cease to regard it as a moral issue. Some adults find their homosexual tendencies degrading: perhaps it is society that is at fault here and not the individual. Some people would find *any* extra-marital sex degrading: it is up to them to decide whether they have good reasons for this view, and whether they should judge other people in the light of their own beliefs. Some people happily have a very wide range of sexual experience: if this is what they really want, and if they always respect the needs of other people, and if they are well enough informed to predict the consequences of their actions – good luck to them! If.

At this point, then, I shall define the first two aims of sex education as:

(1) *to indicate that in sexual relationships, as in any other relationships, other people's feelings and needs are as important as one's own.*

and

(2) *to elucidate the moral implications of this with regard to sexual behaviour.*

But all this would mean nothing in practical terms if young people had no insight (EMP) into the feelings of the opposite sex, or if they were dishonest with themselves about their *own* feelings. It is fairly common, for example, for teenage girls to underestimate the extent to which the way they dress or behave can be sexually provocative; and for boys to underestimate the degree to which a girl can become emotionally involved in what to him is a casual sexual adventure. And both sexes can deceive themselves about their motives: for example, some boys can readily convince themselves that they are in love if this is what the girl seems to want.

The third aim of sex education, therefore, is:

(3) *to promote as much insight as possible into both male and female sexual behaviour, including some awareness of the very wide range of differences between individual members of the same sex.*

We now come to the most obvious aim of sex education, which is:

(4) *to provide adequate factual information* (GIG 1) *about* (a) *relevant aspects of human biology (intercourse, conception, pregnancy, childbirth, contraception, V.D., and so on), and* (b) *the sexual mores of our own and of other societies.*

The less one is factually informed about these matters, the less possible it is to predict the consequences of one's actions in sexual relationships. The dangers of ignorance about contraception or venereal diseases are obvious enough: to overcome them we must either frighten young people into chastity or else see to it that they are well enough informed to *avoid* the dangers. Less obvious, perhaps, are the dangers of ignorance concerning the range of pleasures that can be achieved through intercourse: most people are far too complacent in supposing that 'young people find out these things for themselves'. Most of them probably don't, any more than they would discover for themselves the delights of music and poetry if these subjects were studiously avoided in the curriculum.

It is even more important, however, that people should learn to *communicate* with each other (GIG 2) about their sexual needs. I suspect that even within marriage many people can only communicate with each other at the crude level of a foreigner who goes into a five star hotel knowing only the phrase 'Fish and chips, please'. Young people can scarcely hope for satisfactory relationships if the only language at their disposal (borrowed from magazines or television) is hopelessly inadequate for expressing *their* needs and wishes. All our experiences are enriched if they can be shared – and we need *language* to be able to do this fully: marriages can fail all the more easily if neither partner is capable of talking about his or her feelings. Yet we must expect young people to be inarticulate if they are set no example by either their parents or their teachers.

Perhaps, therefore, the most important aim in sex education is:

(5) *to prepare boys and girls to be able to communicate with each other about their sexual emotions, wishes and needs.*

Finally, following John Wilson's components, the last two aims (relevant to KRAT 1 and 2) will be:

(6) *to foster sensitivity towards those aspects of sexual relationships where moral judgements may be required*

and

(7) *to help young people to be confident enough of their own principles to* act *upon them.*

I will not deny that this is all very idealistic. It will be many years before most schools have any inkling of the extent of their responsibilities in sex education. Currently the situation is abominable*, and we cannot yet hope for much improvement to be brought about by younger teachers, since very few Colleges of Education prepare students actually to *teach* about sex. (One symptom is that the question 'What should be the aims of sex education in schools?' was recently withdrawn from the 'Principles of Education' examination because most of the representatives of the colleges concerned found it 'unsuitable' without giving reasons.)

Nevertheless the time is ripe to develop a 'philosophy of sex education' so that if people agree about its *aims* they can perhaps think more constructively about *methods*. There is no space here

* See my article 'Sex Education in Schools', published in *Let's Teach Them Right*. Pemberton.

to do more than indicate what sort of practical steps are necessary, but I hope that those readers who are interested will be able to supply a lot of details for themselves.

In the first place it should now be apparent that sex education should not appear on the timetable: if it does then there is a real danger that other teachers will 'leave it to the experts' and forget that they all have their own contribution to make. Sex education is a continuous process which starts at birth. Successful relationships within the family are a precondition of successful education within the schools. The 'process education' of the primary school, since its aim is to help children to develop at all levels of their personality, is an essential prelude to successful education during adolescence, when children begin to have relationships which they recognize themselves as being 'sexual', and when a confident sense of personal identity provides a comparatively secure basis for such relationships. At this stage the 'thematic studies' approach would help by making possible the sort of psychological enquiry which seldom finds a place in subject-based education.

There can be no *formula* for the achievement of the seven aims which I have defined, since they are only a dimension of the whole educational process. More specifically, all the practical aspects of moral education that were discussed in the last chapter can be seen to provide the sort of context in which sex education should take place. There are, however, a few points worth making with regard to specific aims.

Aims 1 and 2, concerning the basis of 'sexual morality' are of the sort which can partly be achieved by fairly direct methods, such as open-ended discussion, in the upper part of the secondary school. Most children are not used to the idea that one can have *reasons* for holding moral views, and in my experience it is a great relief to them to see that it is possible to have a reasonable basis for sexual conduct. They tend to reject the popular superstitions and taboos of our society, and the authoritarian pronouncements of unthinking adults, without developing anything in their place except a sloppy sort of liberalism which is too ill-founded to help them in real relationships. But they can be helped to see that one can both be liberal *and* have firm moral principles (e.g. 'It is wrong to get what you want by deceiving people', 'It is wrong to produce unwanted babies').

Aim 4, the provision of factual knowledge, should in *principle* present no problem; though the sad truth is that in fact less than 25 per cent of teenagers leave school with adequate biological knowledge. To my mind, the only controversial issue is how *far* one should give factual information about, for example, sexual techniques or sexual deviations. Of course, in schools of the sort that I described in Chapters Four and Five the teachers would be left in no doubt about what pupils *wanted* to know about sex and in principle this is the best guide to what should be taught.

Lastly, with regard to aims 3 and 5, it is worth asking to what extent they could be achieved by the intelligent use of suitable literature, films, television programmes and drama. I am not suggesting that these media should be used to present a crash course in sex education, but that a suitable selection throughout secondary education would help pupils to achieve insight into their sexual feelings and at the same time to achieve a sense of proportion about them.

Averagely intelligent 15-year-olds, for example, would enjoy the love story of Daphnis and Chloe (Longus) which includes the episode where Daphnis realizes for the first time his sexual ignorance:

> 'But what more can there be,' she asked, 'than kissing and embracing and actually lying down? What do you mean to do when we're lying together naked?'
>
> 'What the rams do to the ewes,' he replied, 'and what the he-goats do to the she-goats. Haven't you noticed that when they've done it the she-goats stop running away from the he-goats and the he-goats stop having the trouble of chasing them? From then on, they graze side by side as if they'd shared some pleasure between them. Apparently what they do is something very sweet which takes away the bitterness of love.'
>
> 'But Daphnis, haven't *you* noticed that the sheep and goats stay standing up? Yet you want me to lie down without any clothes on.'

However, Daphnis had his way. He lay down beside her and stayed there for some time; but not knowing what to do next, he made her get up again and tried imitating the goats. Then, feeling more baffled than ever, he sat down and burst into tears, to think that he knew less about making love than a sheep.'

The Diary of Anne Frank contains some particularly illuminating letters where she is confiding to her imaginary friend about her first, delicate sexual relationship. This material is all the more valuable as it was written by an adolescent and as its honesty is utterly convincing to adolescent readers:

Dear Kitty,
     Do you think that Daddy and Mummy would approve of my sitting and kissing a boy on a divan – a boy of seventeen and a half and a girl of just under fifteen? I don't really think they would, but I must rely on myself over this. It is so quiet and peaceful to lie in his arms and to dream, it is so thrilling to feel his cheek against mine, it is so lovely to know that there is someone waiting for me. But there is indeed a big 'but', because will Peter be content to leave it at this? I haven't forgotten his promise already, but . . . he *is* a boy!
     I know myself that I'm starting very soon, not even fifteen, and so independent already! It's certainly hard for other people to understand, I know almost for certain that Margot would never kiss a boy unless there had been some talk of an engagement or marriage, but neither Peter nor I have anything like that in mind. I'm sure too that Mummy never touched a man before Daddy. What would my girl friends say about it if they knew I lay in Peter's arms, my heart against his chest, my head on his shoulder and with his head against mine!
     Oh, Anne, how scandalous! But honestly, I don't think it is; we are shut up here, shut away from the world, in fear and anxiety, especially just lately. Why then should we who love each other remain apart? Why should we wait until we have reached a suitable age? Why should we bother?
     I have taken it upon myself to look after myself; he would never want to cause me sorrow or pain. Why shouldn't I follow the way my heart leads me, if it makes us both happy? All the same,

Kitty, I believe you can sense that I'm in doubt, I think it must be my honesty which rebels against doing anything on the sly! Do you think it's my duty to tell Daddy what I'm doing? Do you think we should share our secret with a third person? A lot of the beauty would be lost, but would my conscience feel happier? I will discuss it with 'him'.

Oh, yes, there's still so much I want to talk to him about, for I don't see the use of only just cuddling each other. To exchange our thoughts, that shows confidence, and faith in each other; we would both be sure to profit by it!

Yours, Anne

The quality of her feelings might usefully be compared with those of Billy Liar when he was trying to seduce the 'witch' in a churchyard, or with those of Holden Cauldfield in *The Catcher in the Rye*.

A bold but sensitive choice of good literature can do a lot to help teenagers to become aware that there is such a thing as *style* in sexual relationships; and the same thing applies to films except that there are very few which are honest about adolescent sexual relationships. Perhaps sixth-formers or students in College of Education could make a project of listing suitable materials: if they did, I would be delighted to hear their opinions.

ten

Religious Education

In Chapter Eight I was able to write with some confidence about the aims of moral education mainly because the concepts of 'morality' and 'a morally educated person' are ones which I find intelligible. R.E. presents more difficult problems, however: 'religion' is a very obscure concept, and I frankly have no idea what it means to be 'a religiously educated person'. Nevertheless, these problems must be discussed, for if there is any subject traditionally associated with the imparting of values then this is certainly R.E.

The word 'religion', to an anthropologist*, usually means 'A belief in spiritual beings'; but this is not altogether satisfactory since this description would exclude the theology of Buddhism and include a belief in fairies at the bottom of the garden. Some philosophers have felt that the essence of a religion lies in its *ethical* meaning; but in fact the connection between religion and morality is extremely obscure, as we saw on page 65. Matthew Arnold described religion as 'morality tinged with emotion' – a concept which does perhaps remind us that actively *caring* about people can help one to behave morally towards them. But one can care about people without being religious.

Many theologians find the emotional aspect the most important one, basing religion on a 'sense of awe in the face of the numinous'; but others would claim to be religious without having had any experience of this sort. Others again try to combine the sense of sacred awe with the definition of religion as an all-embracing system for understanding the 'nature of the universe' or the

* I am here drawing on an article by Mary Douglas in *New Society,* 12th March, 1970.

'meaning of life'; yet it is very difficult to see precisely what sort of understanding of these things is provided, for example, by modern Christianity (since Christians are as likely as any other people to disagree among themselves about theological, spiritual and moral issues).

In view of the complexity of the subject I shall therefore try to do without a definition of 'religion', but in order to get anywhere at all I shall suppose for the purposes of this chapter that 'being religious' (in our society) usually involves:

(a) believing in an omnipotent spiritual being
(b) having certain experiences directly related to the existence and nature of such a being, and
(c) being influenced in one's way of living by (a) and (b).

I shall also make the large assumption that the only possible basis for *believing* in such a spiritual being (as opposed to *hypothesizing* one) is either having 'religious' experience or trusting such experience in other people.

Now just as one can be a 'moral' person (in some sense of that word) without being 'morally educated' to any great extent, so presumably can one be 'religious' without being 'religiously educated'. Moral education leads the 'moral' person to examine his beliefs and attitudes more closely, to discover their logical status, to be more flexible in their application. Presumably *religious* education leads to an examination of religious beliefs and attitudes: what is the basis of these beliefs? what *facts* are relevant? how should these beliefs affect the way in which I live?

There is, however, an important dissimilarity between the two. Nearly everyone has some sort of 'moral' experience in the sense that he often has to decide what he *ought* to do, that he has feelings of obligation, duty, remorse, and so on, and has some concept of how to use the words 'good' and 'bad' in a moral sense. How such moral awareness is first achieved is a very complex question, but no one doubts that it *exists*; if it did not children would not be morally educable.

But whether children have *religious* experience is a much more puzzling question, since there is no general agreement about what constitutes such experience or even about whether the expression is meaningful. (I am assuming here that we need not use the word 'religious' for attitudes, feelings or ideas which are simply *copied* from adults.)

Therefore, again without attempting a definition, I am going to simplify the problem by arbitrarily choosing four popular lines of thought about religious experience to see what light they might throw on the nature of religious education.

1. 'So-called religious experience can be explained in natural terms so we have no good reason for believing in the supernatural.' – in which case the aim of R.E. is merely to study *facts* about what certain people say they believe and how their beliefs affect their behaviour. In other words R.E. would consist of various topics such as the history of world religions, the sociology of religious groups, the psychology of religious experience, the systems of ethics associated with certain religions, and so on.

2. 'What is loosely called "religious experience" is a life-enhancing, unpredictable sense of wonder, awe, astonishment or joy, characterised by a feeling of contact with a supernatural being. Such a being may exist, but such experience is not *proof*.' – in which case the aim of R.E. would be a study of such experiences in other people and in oneself, and a consideration of what significance and value such experiences have.

3. ' "Religious experience" consists of certain states of mind (which to a certain degree can predictably be induced by prayer, meditation or other means) in which one can attain a deeper insight into certain aspects of the universe. Such insight could only be gained by contact with a supernatural power, and therefore the experience is proof that such a power exists.' – in which case R.E. involves (*a*) a study of a wide range of such experiences (their nature and consequences, and the circumstances in which they occurred), and (*b*) a study of the implications of such experience (what do we really learn from them? why should we trust them? how should our lives be affected?).

4. 'Some sorts of religious experience are more illuminating than others. In particular, we have sufficient evidence of a benign, omniscient creator about whom we can learn from the life of Jesus Christ.' – in which case the aims of R.E. are (a) to study records of such experience, (b) to find out everything possible about the life of Christ, (c) to consider why the life of Christ should throw light on the nature of God, and (d) to help people to live in a way which seems desirable in the light of (a), (b), and (c).

The first line of thought is, of course, the one most likely to appeal to humanists. Nobody can deny that large areas of history would be incomprehensible if one were ignorant of religious movements, that many of Man's greatest artistic achievements would remain obscure, that our understanding of other peoples would be diminished, and that we could not hope to grasp the nature of our own cultural heritage. Even so, it can be an arid line of thought – as arid as teaching the history of literature and the terminology of literary criticism to those who have no appreciation of poetry because they derive no 'aesthetic experience' from it. Such an approach to religion could count as *education* only if teachers helped their pupils towards an imaginative insight into the spirit of, say, Christianity and Buddhism. This point was expressed well by Professor Ninian Smart*:

> The spirit of . . .? Eyebrows may here be raised. What is the real possibility of conveying the spirit of a faith through its history? Here we touch on a crucial problem in the teaching of the subject.
>
> One of the recurrent defects of textbooks (of some textbooks) is that value-judgements of the wrong kind creep in. For instance, Indian religions are presented as 'world-negating', 'pessimistic' and so on. Certain of the descriptive terms we tend to use, conditioned by our own cultural and religious heritage, are laden with judgements. Every time some external value-judgement of this kind occurs, it involves a betrayal of what I shall call the 'principle of intentionality'. Let me explain this briefly as follows.

* 'Comparative Study of Religion in Schools', published in *Religious Education* (The Religious Education Association, New York).

In describing a human activity, we only describe fully and correctly if we include in the description the meaning the activity has for the person or persons participating. It is strictly a misdescription if I say that a person is praying to a statue, if he conceives himself as praying to Vishnu. Thus description must include reference to the intentions and beliefs, etc., of those who engage in them. This is what I mean by the principle of intentionality.

The task then of a description in religion is in part to bring out the meanings and values present to the participants. This task is obscured and frustrated when external meanings and values are imposed upon them. Thus, in an important sense, the study of a religion involves *presenting* that faith, and so the exercise frequently involves considerable powers of sensitivity and imagination. . . . In principle, then, a major result of studying religion is to be able to give a sympathetic and 'intentional' description or presentation of a faith or faiths.

If one *does* favour this line of approach to R.E., however, it seems to me that it would be inappropriate to have R.E. as a *subject* on the timetable, at least until pupils are 15 or 16. In practical terms I suggest that the best results would be achieved by the 'thematic studies' approach (see Chapter Five), whereby different disciplines (such as History, Geography, Art, Music, Literature, Drama and Social Studies) provided evidence, and whereby outside specialists were invited, if necessary, to contribute to the 'core' lessons. The occasional study of a religious theme, in this way, would almost certainly produce more desirable results that would be possible for the R.E. teacher who normally sees a particular class for only two periods a week or even less. Perhaps readers would like to consider what sort of themes would be appropriate at various levels of secondary education.

The second line of thought ('religious' experience as an unpredictable sense of awe) may attract teachers who believe that all education should start from the experience of the child. Unfortunately it is difficult to see in what sense *religion* is involved and, indeed, to see specifically what sort of education would be relevant. This is not to say that the concept is *mistaken*: indeed, it seems to me that in primary schools it would be much better to get rid of anything called R.E. and to concentrate exclusively on the sort of work described in Chapter Four. The more imaginative, stimulating and varied the work of the child, the more likely it is that he will be rich in *all* kinds of experience, including the numinous ones; for a sense of awe is more likely to be aroused by walking on hills, by seeing the birth of an animal, by turning clay on a wheel, by making music, writing poetry, dancing – than by studying the lives of good people or by saying obscure prayers under conditions of extreme physical discomfort.

This difference is symbolized in Roman Catholic primary schools I have visited where excellent teaching has led to a classroom, full of evidence of the children's creativity (paintings, models, collages all bursting with life), in which the only tawdry things to be seen were a wretched plastic Madonna, a sickly painting of 'Christ the Storyteller' and a printed list of '40 Things I Will Do To Show My Love For Jesus This Lent'.

When we come to the third and fourth lines of thought (religious experience as mystical revelation) we have to face the enormous problem that there is no domain of publicly justifiable religious knowledge. We can safely teach *about* beliefs – because what people believe is a matter of fact. But we cannot justifiably set out to *instil* beliefs. In other areas of school work there is no doubt of the validity of the vast majority of what is taught, and furthermore there are accepted grounds and criteria in terms of which that validity can be defended. But at present this does not appear to apply to religion, for although religious believers make claims to truth and knowledge they differ radically about both the nature and the basis of their beliefs; and there are no agreed public tests whereby the true and false can be distinguished.

It therefore seems quite wrong (at least in State schools) to present as fact religious views which at present cannot be shown to be true; and it seems even less justifiable to involve children in forms of worship (such as prayer and hymn-singing) which are only meaningful if the children already share the beliefs which are implicit in such worship. Some teachers claim that such involvement in worship is justified on the grounds that 'at least it gives children the *opportunity* for religious experience, which they can then evaluate as they wish'; but it is not far from this point of view to suggest that children should also be given L.S.D. in case *that* experience proved valuable.

But not only is the fourth line of thought positively immoral (if current Christian ideas are presented as facts): it is also dangerous. For whereas *rationality* can never be out of date, current fashions in religion can later seem very embarrassing, and as irrelevant to newer religious concepts as the following extract from a Children's Encyclopedia of the sort read by our grandparents:

> The missionary, who fulfils the command of Jesus to his disciples, Go ye into all the world and preach the Gospel to every creature, cheerfully leaves his native land, his home and his friends, to spend his life where there is no civilization, no comfort or safety, to dwell with dark-skinned men who worship ugly idols and are given to superstitious and cruel practices. The missionary is the pioneer – the first in the field; he makes it possible for trade to follow in his steps; for the natives will believe in the white men who come on business, because they respect and trust the one who has been their good friend and taught them to live rightly.

To take a more serious example, we do not now suppose that it was good for people to be presented with Genesis as the literal truth about the Creation; though if they could also think rationally about what *mattered* in their religion it was easy for them to move towards a different concept of the meaning of Genesis without their faith being impaired in any way. In the same way it seems quite possible that, if it were discovered that the Gospels had no factual basis, many Christians would quickly come to terms with the new situation by reinterpreting the Gospels as a symbolic expression of true ideas about God.

It seems, therefore, that the aims of religious education should be (*a*) to teach *about* religious beliefs, and (*b*) to help people to think *rationally* about the beliefs and emotions that they have.

We have already seen that (*a*) is an essential ingredient of education which, for maximum value, involves helping pupils towards

H

an imaginative insight into religious beliefs. I shall now conclude this chapter with some comments about (*b*).

To think rationally about religious beliefs involves asking questions such as the following: What distinguishes a religious experience from any other kind of experience? How can one tell if apparent encounters with God are real or hallucinatory? If one simply feels *committed* to certain beliefs, what is there in that commitment that guarantees the truth of the beliefs? Why should one trust the evidence of the Bible? What sort of evidence *is* given by the Bible? On what basis can we claim to have some understanding of the existence and nature of God? What is the connection between *religious* judgements and *moral* judgements? What constitutes *proof* in religious matters?

As is the case with questions of sexual morality it can be a great relief to teenagers to find that religion can be discussed rationally. At the simplest level, those inclined towards atheism or agnosticism can be led into discussion of the grounds on which they reject theism and of alternative ways of considering popular questions about the nature of the universe (e.g. 'Did life evolve by chance?'); while those who are militantly Christian can be persuaded to consider the basis of their views and to ask more searching questions about their implications in terms of behaviour towards other people.

At a more advanced level, however, we should expect sixth-formers to be kept in touch with recent developments in theological thinking which may ultimately revolutionize our concept of the nature of religious education.

Two such developments are discussed by Professor Paul Hirst in an article called 'Morals, Religion and the Maintained Schools'.* Having discussed the attempts of the neo-Thomists to reinterpret the traditional proofs of God's existence in a way which will stand up to contemporary philosophical criticism, he goes on to discuss a line of thought popularized by Professor Ninian Smart:

> At the same time a number of philosophers less happy about the

* Published in the *British Journal of Educational Studies*.

traditional categories have sought to characterize afresh the meaning and truth of religious propositions. To them religious statements are attempts to talk intelligibly about certain aspects of man's natural experience, his experience in everyday contexts, not simply that in such specifically religious contexts as, say, church worship. The view is that religious discourse picks out man's awareness that the universe is not self-explanatory, that human experience and knowledge are set in ultimate mystery and this awareness breaks in on man in a great variety of circumstances. Some such experiences we have come to call numinous, others we regard as more mystical in character. Religious language is then regarded not as telling us facts about the inner nature of the mystery, but as attempts in parabolic or metaphysical language to relate and make intelligible these experiences. The only language we have is a language whose meaning is closely tied to our experience of the finite world. When it comes to understanding this area of mystery and to answering limiting questions about our experience of it, then our language becomes figurative. Most developed religions, for instance, have come to speak of experiences of mystery as experiences of a 'person' but this is simply an analogy or picture by which to characterize the experiences. When it comes to tests for the truth of religious statements, the point must be the adequacy of the pictures in making sense of the range and circumstances of the experiences. The tests must therefore necessarily be more on the lines of those appropriate for the 'truth' of literary works rather than those for, say, scientific theories.

. . . it does not seem at all impossible that an agreed rational basis for at least some religious claims might be found. In so far as a domain of religious knowledge can be established, the frontiers of the content of education appropriate to maintained schools must, it seems to me, be moved so as to include it. The subject would then take its place alongside others in the schools. It would be taught necessarily as a mode of our understanding of human experience – the pupils' own and others – and the validated knowledge would be set in a context in which the principles and tests on which it rests would be taught as well. The nearest parallel in method of approach might well be that in the teaching of literature.

As Professor Hirst admits, this line of thought may just be crystal-gazing. But it does make it clear that there is a lot of very hard thinking to be done before religious *education* (as opposed to instruction about religions) can be achieved as confidently as education in other modes of thinking.

Interlude 4

THE sun shone brightly on Monica Perkins' last day as a school-girl. To get out of bed she had to clamber over one of her mother's West Indian boy-friends – who had turned up late the night before only to find that Mrs Perkins' 'steady' was at home on leave and who had therefore taken up the only available bed space, being too drunk to leave the house.

She mindlessly ate some cornflakes. She wondered what to wear for school: one of her two dresses was in the wash, and the other she had been wearing overnight, for she had gone to bed fully dressed. It would have to be sweater and jeans, and this would mean another boring lecture from Mrs Bryce.

Although it was still only nine o'clock the sun was blazing hot. Her clothes, still damp from the wardrobe, began to irritate her skin; so she went into a small copse at the edge of the cemetery, laid out her sweater and jeans to dry, ate half a dozen peppermint creams, and fell into a deep sleep. When she woke up, feeling rather sick, the church clock was striking two o'clock. 'Oh Christ,' she thought in a moment of panic, 'now Bricey really will have kittens.' Then she remembered that it was her last day at school. Tomorrow she would be beyond the long arm of Bricey for ever. Why had it been important to go to school today? – yes, she was supposed to queue up outside the Head's room to collect her testimonial. Well, they could stuff their testimonial: there was no one at home who could read it.

For a while she toyed with the idea of sneaking into the end-of-term Assembly that always began as soon as all the teachers had fiddled their registers to balance for the whole year. She could just make it if she hurried.

The class teachers would be filing their pupils into the Hall while the Deputy Head snapped at their heels like a sheep-dog. The Head would be wearing his gown, and would spend the first half-hour saying that he wanted this to be a short Assembly so that everyone could get home. Somebody at the back would then make a stupid comment, the Head would blow his top, and the whole school would return to their classrooms to repeat the operation all over again.

The R.E. teacher, Mr Daniels (Dan, Dan, the Assembly Man), would give a stupid talk about the temptations facing school-leavers ('When you begin to mix with Workers in Shops and Factories you will come across Ideas both New and Dangerous'). Then there would be an endless succession of prize-giving (from each class one for Success, one for Endeavour, and one for being a Creep). The biggest and best prizes would go to 5A because they wore school uniform, did homework, and could play games since they didn't have jobs on Saturdays.

A ragged singing of 'Lord, dismiss us – ' interrupted by the music teacher crying 'STOP, I didn't hear the first syllable' – and then a slow dismissal while teachers scattered to various parts of the school to make sure that nothing was broken or stolen.

Time for the leavers to say goodbye. Well, Monica would have liked to say goodbye to Mr Bennett – he was a good sport – and to Miss Gifkins – a bit simple, but very nice. And . . .

The effort of thinking in the hot sun was too much. She turned over on to her stomach and went back to sleep.

eleven

Education and Reform

I BEGAN this book by saying that the values of a given society are inevitably reflected in the kind of education that it provides: 'for the schools are preparing their pupils to take a place in that society, and they must teach subjects that are valued in that society by methods which are approved of in that society'.

This is only part of the truth, however, for the values of a society change over the years and it seems probable that education is one of the many factors which are instrumental in *causing* that change. In other words, education not only reflects the values of the society: it perhaps helps to modify them. But if so, how?

For a start we can dismiss the idea of society being deliberately changed (for better or for worse) by a sort of conspiracy among teachers. Even if it were conceivable that all teachers agreed on what sort of changes they wanted to make in society (or were told by the government what changes were required), and even if they managed to effect those aims, such a process would be one of indoctrination – not education. This crude concept of 'education' as reform is one which may have its attraction in a totalitarian state but not in a democracy where (however one defines 'democracy') no minority can be justified in imposing its own set of values upon the majority of people. Of course there have been attempts to use 'education' in this sort of way in our own society: the working classes have been 'educated' to 'know their place'; people have been 'educated' to hold certain religious views; and nowadays, more fashionably, there are many 'liberal' teachers who use equally pernicious methods of fostering 'liberal' views in their pupils. But none of this will count as *education*, and some philosophers have indeed drawn the conclusion that by its very nature education cannot be *used* as an instrument of reform.

I would not quarrel with this point of view; but it is still worth looking at what sort of connection does exist between education and changes in social values. We know that existing values *cause* certain things to happen in education, but is the converse true, i.e. can education cause changes in values?

I think it is reasonable to say that there is a tendency in our society to value 'equality'. We are prone to say that, in some sense, 'all people are equal' or 'have equal rights' or should have 'equality of opportunity'. (And from this certain other popular values follow logically, such as 'freedom of speech'.) We do not suppose that all people are the *same* (i.e. have the same abilities, wishes and needs) but many of us do suppose that they should have an equal chance of developing their abilities as far as *possible*, and of satisfying their wishes and needs as far as is compatible with the well-being of other people.

Now if we value 'equality' along these lines, there are many consequences educationally; and the most obvious of these is that everyone should have the same chance of being educated. For this to happen even in the loosest sense, education must be free (or most people couldn't afford it) and compulsory over a certain age span (or many parents would deprive their children of it).

There are also less obvious consequences, and the less obvious they are the more controversial they must be. Here are some examples which I shall put in question form:

1. Some children start at a disadvantage for all sorts of reasons such as (*a*) having parents who are uneducated and hostile to education, (*b*) belonging to a social class where expectation of academic success is very low, (*c*) living in areas with poor educational facilities, and (*d*) being handicapped physically or mentally.

To treat these children 'equally' do we need to discriminate positively in their favour (e.g. by spending more money in 'high priority areas' to improve facilities and attract more teachers, by speeding up the provision of nursery education to compensate for poor home environment, by providing special schools for the grossly handicapped)?

2. We know that if one 'streams' children, they tend to make the sort of progress *expected* of those streams. Children labelled 'C'-stream, therefore, do not in practice have an equal chance of success even if their 'potential' has been underestimated.

To provide equality of opportunity, must we therefore abandon streaming in all its forms – i.e. abandon the Grammar/Secondary Modern division, and abandon streaming within the school and even within the class?

3. Exceptionally gifted children also need special provisions if they are to have an equal opportunity of developing their abilities as far as possible. Again, 'positive discrimination' may be necessary.

How can this be achieved within the comprehensive system? (I am personally convinced that it *can* be.)

4. The comprehensive system will not provide equality of opportunity (either at primary or secondary level) if some schools are mainly middle class and others are not. Middle-class children start at an advantage because of the higher level of literacy in their background, and a higher level of parental co-operation which would soon result in the middle class schools being better equipped than other schools.

How can we avoid 'streaming' schools by social class?

5. The kind of education provided can accentuate (and falsify) apparent differences between pupils' ability. For example, if a school values only academic and sporting success, children who are unsuccessful in these fields may be made to feel totally inferior as human beings.

How can schools genuinely show that they value other virtues in their pupils, that they care about educating them as *people* rather than as units in an elaborate competition?

6. If teachers believe in equality (and hold the attitude PHIL) what should the consequences be in terms of the sort of moral education

that they provide? In particular, does it follow that they should foster in their pupils the ability to be constructively critical of existing social values? Can people be 'equal' if they have to rely on other people's moral judgements?

Now supposing for the sake of argument that I am right in saying that believing in equality entails (a) genuinely comprehensive education, and (b) the sort of moral education described in Chapter 8; then so far I have simply illustrated the uncontroversial point that social values have certain consequences educationally. But what of the converse? Would the sort of education I have described ultimately lead to changes in social values?

One can, of course, only make wild guesses. Indeed, if one *could* accurately predict the consequences then my whole argument would be invalidated; for *successful* teachers should expect that some of their pupils will ultimately be capable of better judgements than they themselves.

Nevertheless it does seem likely that, in the first stages of the 'revolution', the present sort of class structure would disintegrate. I am not naïve enough to suppose that this would result *merely* from comprehensivization, for poor comprehensive schools can doubtless further entrench class consciousness. On the other hand it does seem likely that grammar schools perpetuate class distinctions by creaming off bright middle-class children, giving them the best educational resources (small classes, etc.) and sending them on to further education – which in turn leads to their having more than their fair share of power and therefore the ability to perpetuate a society favourable to their own middle-class offspring.

The compulsory introduction of comprehensive schools could in principle help to end this state of affairs, and place further education and power in the hands of a wider cross-section of the people. We could then no longer expect those with the power to reform society automatically to share the tastes, ambitions and prejudices reflected in traditional middle-class mores.

I have heard some people argue that this state of affairs would be better because at last the 'sturdy morality of the working classes' would come into its own. This is nonsense. The working classes haven't got 'a morality': if one tries to draw a distinction between 'working-class morality' and 'middle-class morality' all one does is to list differences between their different habits of thought, prejudices and tastes. In other words, one is talking about *mores*, not *morality*; and so far all that the revolution would have achieved is to give us a new power structure reflecting one set of prejudices rather than another. This would doubtless be *fairer* in one limited sense, but there is no reason to suppose that it would be *better*.

I am looking further ahead, however, to a revolution of a quite different sort; for education does not simply give people more power – it extends them as *people*. It gives them the mental equipment to recognize habit and prejudice for what they are, to think rationally about their way of life and their moral attitudes.

And this suggests a more important kind of revolution – one which could not have occurred at any previous point in history. It is only for a tiny fragment of human evolution that societies have existed where *everyone* gets some sort of education in schools beyond the critical age of 12 or 13 when they can learn to think for themselves. It is only during the last few years that we have begun to put into practice (to some degree) the concepts of education that I have described in this book. And we are only just beginning to explore the implications of getting people to think for themselves about morality. What would be the ultimate consequences, after several generations, of an all-out effort to take education seriously, to put into practice all our good intentions? Would the result simply be that *more* people accepted the value of equality? Or would people have quite different ideas of what equality entails? Or would they perhaps not value equality at all, and develop a different sort of class structure?

There is, of course, no way of knowing. We are not using education to create the kind of society we ourselves value. We can only start with basic moral values which it seems rational to accept, and then decide what sort of educational process can best embody them.

But a process conceived in these terms will enable people to generate their own values, and these in turn will throw new light on education itself. This interaction is as inevitable as it will be endless.

Don't turn the rat cage to the wall

MOST of the books in this series include some comments on relevant vocational training, but since the various routes into the teaching profession are so well documented I shall confine this section to three pieces of practical advice aimed at those who wish to become teachers.

First, and most important, do something else before you embark on professional training. If you are going to study for a Teacher's Certificate or a Dip. Ed., get a job in Woolworth's or on a building site for at least a year beforehand. It doesn't matter what kind of job it is so long as it's nothing to do with teaching. For one thing, you may have forty years of education ahead, and you don't want to spend *all* your life in schools; and for another thing it is just as well to broaden your experience of the background of future pupils. A year in an unskilled job will teach you more than all the sociology lectures you will get at College.

Second, don't go into the teaching profession if you are a nice, respectable, dull person who can't think of anything else to do. Take up a job where, by the nature of your work, you aren't *compelled* to bore other people to death.

Lastly, be prepared always to regard your pupils as your equals, and don't be surprised that they can read your mind better than you can yourself. Don't, therefore, read them poems which don't appeal to you but which you think *they* ought to like. Don't ask them to write stories or essays that you couldn't be bothered to write yourself. Never refuse to answer sincere questions because you don't think they ought to know the answers. Don't be afraid to admit that you are ignorant. And *never* turn the rat cage to the wall.

Further Reading

A. *General Introduction to Philosophy*

A serious study of the philosophy of education must begin with some general understanding of the analytical approach used by contemporary British philosophers.

The simplest introductions are:

Philosophy, John Wilson, Heinemann, 1968
Moral Thinking, John Wilson, Heinemann, 1970

At a more advanced level, I suggest the following as starting points:

The Problems of Philosophy, Bertrand Russell, London, 1912
Language, Truth and Logic, A. J. Ayer, London, 1946

In the very relevant field of moral philosophy, two outstanding works are:

The Language of Morals, R. M. Hare, Oxford, 1952
Freedom and Reason, R. M. Hare, Oxford, 1956

B. *The Philosophy of Education*

The clearest short work on this subject is probably:

An Introduction to the Philosophy of Education, D. J. O'Connor, Routledge, 1957

Good examples of analytical techniques being applied to problems in education are:

The Concept of Education, ed. R. S. Peters, Allen & Unwin
Ethics and Education, R. S. Peters, Allen & Unwin, 1966

Aims in Education, ed. T. H. B. Hollins, Manchester, 1964

On more specific issues, important books are:

An Introduction to Moral Education, John Wilson *et al,* Penguin, 1969

Education and the Concept of Mental Health, John Wilson, Routledge, 1968

C. *The Sociology of Education*

Education and Society, A. K. C. Ottoway, Routledge, 1962

This book contains an excellent bibliography which would lead students on to a deeper study of any issues in which they were particularly interested.

For a lucid study of research techniques used by sociologists I suggest:

Social Research, Michael Schofield, Heinemann, 1969

D. *The Psychology of Education*

The most popular general introduction is probably:

An Introduction to Educational Psychology, E. Stones, Methuen, 1966

Again, there is a very useful reading list:

Child Development, Norman Williams, Heinemann, 1969

is an unusually clear analysis of the nature of theories in this area. Of the 'classics', those particularly valuable to students are:

The Language and Thought of the Child, Jean Piaget, Routledge

The Child's Conception of Number, Jean Piaget, Routledge

Child Care and the Growth of Love, John Bowlby, Penguin, 1965

The Child, the Family, and the Outside World, D. W. Winnicott, Penguin, 1964

The most lucid writer on contemporary psychoanalytical theory is probably Charles Rycroft, and I strongly recommend:

Anxiety and Neurosis, C. Rycroft, Penguin
Psychoanalysis Observed, ed. C. Rycroft, Constable, 1966

Of particular interest in relation to Chapter Four is:

'Symbolism and Its Relation to the Primary and Secondary Process' published in *Imagination and Reality,* Hogarth Press, 1968

The writings of Freud remain unsurpassed for clarity. Again in relation to Chaper Four the following is particularly relevant:

Splitting of the Ego in the Defensive process (1938), Standard Edition, Vol. 23, Hogarth Press, 1964.

E. *The History of Education*

Starting points for the further study of all major educational thinkers, from Plato to Dewey, will be found in:

A Short History of Educational Ideas, Curtis and Boultwood, U.T.P., 1954

This book is not, however, very acute philosophically. By far the best philosophical background is provided by:

The History of Western Philosophy, Bertrand Russell, London, 1946

F. *Comparative Education*

A good book to start with is:

Comparative Education, Nicholas Hans, Routledge